Wake Up
to the
Dream
of a
Debt-Free Life

Dr. C Marie

Kiernan, Cindy Marie
 Wake Up to the Dream of a Debt-Free Life
 by Dr. C Marie
 ISBN 978-1-59285-849-1

Editor's note
This publication is not intended as a substitute for advice from CFP professionals.

Cover Design by Vicki Hughes, Design|From A to V
Cover Photo by Mallory, Capturing Hope

DEDICATION

For Mom

who loves... unconditionally.

CONTENTS

Wake Up to the Dream of a Debt-Free Life

ACKNOWLEDGEMENTS

As I considered writing this book, I kept thinking about how blessed I have been with a career in the field of education. The amazing students, faculty, administrators, parents and colleagues I met along the way have been a part of my life and hold a special place in my heart.

For my mom, Agnes: I offer sincere appreciation for your never-ending belief in me through not only challenging times, but also extraordinary times in my life.

For my entire family and beloved family friend, Frank: I extend sincere gratitude for the encouragement, love, and support during my creation of Puzzle Pieces to Pathway, LLC and the writing of *Wake Up to the Dream of a Debt-Free Life.*

For my two sisters, Kathryn and Barbara, and their husbands, Billy and Bobby: Your love and deep appreciation for me as part of your families allow me to experience great happiness as I spend time with you and your children. Your balance of faith, generosity, and love has been what I needed through many seasons of life.

For my nieces, Whitney, Mallory and Ansley, my nephew, Tyler, and my great nephew, Beckham: I have witnessed your lives from birth to current day. Being an aunt has brought me immense joy at a depth no words can express.

For my great nephew, Beckham: You and your mom, Ansley, have brought our family much happiness in the months since your birth. We love you!

For my extended family: Thank you for wonderful childhood memories.

For my friends: You are a group of kind, supportive, loving, gracious, talented and humorous women and men. We have experienced life together, be it for a season, decades, or a lifetime. Thank you.

For Leslie: Our paths crossed as we began teaching at Mountain Park ES. We have walked through a wide range of life experiences together. I sincerely thank you and Dan for including me in your family's celebrations, holidays, and events throughout our friendship.

For Lesa: Having a friend of 50+ years is one of life's special gifts. Your friendship throughout our teenage years and into adulthood has meant the world to me. I admire you not only for your strength and courage, but also your deep love of family.

For Becky and Phyllis: Our deep conversations throughout the past decade, as I have grown in faith, contributed immensely to my journey. Becky, in 2009-10, you gave me a book of inspirational quotes I placed on my desk at SAE. To this day, I attribute much of my decision to move to the next phase of my career- that of teaching at the university level- to a quote in the book... *She believed she could, so she did*. Thank you.

For my professional accountability partners, Kathy and Karen: Meeting with you two accomplished, professional Christian women to discuss our goals and aspirations has "held my feet to the fire" as we strive to contribute to the world around us. Thank you.

For Catherine and Whitney: Thank you for your input during the final stages of the writing of this book.

For the pastors, authors, and speakers who greatly influenced my journey: Thank you for sharing your gifts and talents with the world.

PREFACE

I began writing *Wake Up to the Dream of a Debt-Free Life* after becoming free of debt and forming my company, Puzzle Pieces to Pathway, LLC. During the past two years as I have compiled my notes for this book, interviewed adults of different ages, backgrounds, and marital status, I consistently revisited these quotes and scripture which offered guidance and encouragement during my journey.

You were designed by the Giver of Life to give your life away.

-Andy Stanley
What Makes You Happy

*You cannot be spiritually free
and financially bound.*
-Larry Burkett

So, from the age of five to about twenty, religion to me was a matter of 'you do this, and you don't do that, and you do your best to walk the straight line.'... But once I was on my own, my faith became something very personal. ... I came to think of God as more of a gracious friend who was accompanying me on this journey, a friend who wanted to carry my burdens and speak into my life and shape me into who I really was and who I would become. ...And as I did that, something shifted in me. I started owning who I am, realizing that I was unique, and that God had a unique purpose for me.

-Joanna Gaines
The Magnolia Story (p.44)

If therefore the Son makes you free,
you shall be free indeed.

John 8:36
New American Standard
Bible

INTRODUCTION

As you open *Wake Up to the Dream of a Debt-Free Life*, most likely you open it with hope. Hope for inspiration as you face your own personal struggles with debt. Hope for sharing this book with a friend or loved one who is seeking support and encouragement. Hope in the belief that life *can* be fulfilling during the journey toward debt-free living.

Perhaps you have read a book about money management and given thought to tackling debt, but you simply could not get started. Picking up this book reflects your desire to create a pathway for success- *your* pathway. Congratulations.

I wrote *Wake Up to the Dream of a Debt-Free Life* to encourage you to begin the journey wherever you are. People of all ages, career paths, and circumstances have begun the journey toward debt-free living. Whatever the reason, wherever you are, you can take the first step on your pathway toward success. Now. Today. Go ahead. Turn the page. You can do this!

Chapter 1

The Dream

Following a busy day of moving into my new loft condo, I crawled into bed, and closed my eyes to fall asleep. Instead, my mind began to race. You know how that is. Even though you are exhausted and in need of sleep, thoughts about your day, week, or life emerge. Thoughts about this new move floated through my mind as a feeling of excitement swept over me.

What a great location! Overlooking Main Street in a town filled with restaurants, boutiques, coffee shops, and parks, my condo had the conveniences of life in this trendy, multi-use community and I was determined I would make this my best move yet. *Talk about convenient parking!* I had a parking garage below, so I could park my car on Friday afternoon, and there would be no need to drive until Sunday morning. Even then, I could hardly call it a drive as my church was less than two miles away. To top it off, who wouldn't want an easy commute to work driving opposite traffic with an incredibly beautiful drive along backroads, to boot? For a quick second, it seemed as if my dream had come true! *New York City living... in the suburbs of Atlanta, GA,* I softly exclaimed as I closed my eyes again, this time with the intent of falling fast asleep.

Instead, my eyes suddenly popped opened. Frozen, I stared at the ceiling. Not the chilly, need-more-covers type of frozen, but the "thinking about the amount of money I owed" type of frozen! You may have experienced a similar feeling. A rush of heat throughout your body as you think about debt. A sweaty upper lip, perhaps? A heavy heart?

At that very moment, the term, *hopeless*, seemed to be the most accurate descriptor of my state of finances. Hopeless is

1

not a word I use to describe any other part of my life. I have always been committed to working hard and I deeply treasure family and friends. But now, thinking about finances, *hopeless* seemed to be the only word to suffice. *How could I have made another move without considering a plan for managing finances? Yikes! What have I done?* I thought of family and friends I so deeply treasure and thought, *No way! No way will I let mismanagement of finances be part of my legacy.*

This condo served as my 14th residence since college graduation. I had experience renting apartments, buying and selling homes, and taking out second mortgages. (More about this point later.) For ten years, I had been making bare minimum monthly payments on my $92,000 student loan. This massive amount was the total loan amount for my master's and doctorate degrees. I assumed full responsibility for these loans. I signed for them. They were on me. After a decade of making payments, the balance was reduced to approximately $76,000. *Diligently making monthly payments of $537.08 for ten years had only reduced my original loan amount by $16,000! Really?* During these years I viewed my student loans as an investment. After all, I would not have wished for any other career. I truly loved teaching and was thankful for a rewarding career. *Because I love my work, the loan was...or is... or always will be worth it,* I told myself. I believe this area of life, teaching, is an area I "got right." Such a mindset had been my justification for the outrageous student loan payment each month.

However, the credit card and bank loan debt... another story!

Back to the moment of dawning! Frozen, still staring at the ceiling, I could see the lights from Main Street gently shining through my windows as if to comfort me. The lights, however, seemed to spotlight the numbers dancing in my head. Working mentally with round numbers, I could "see" the amounts of

2

money I owed. Yes, $76,000 in student loan debt, more than $49,000 in credit card debt, credit union loan debt, and bank loan debt, as well as approximately $16,000 in car loan debt. Cha-ching! My mental calculator was smoking! The sum, totaling more than $140,000, appeared to be stamped on the ceiling of my new condo in size 95 font! Yes, you read the number correctly. I had accumulated debt in an amount exceeding $140,000, excluding my new condo mortgage. How could this amount possibly be explained?

For those of you who manage money well and learned to budget at an early age, the answer is obvious. If you are reading this book, perhaps with the hope of sharing it with a family member or friend in need, you are commenting, "I know what happened! You *spent* more than you *earned*!" With this book in hand, others of you, however, are thinking, "I am right there with you, C Marie! I get it! I, too, am in a financial mess and have accumulated a ridiculous amount of debt."

As I would for a friend, I tried to console myself with positive thoughts. *A great condo, wonderful job and colleagues, loving family and friends, awesome pastor and church... everything will work out.*

In my dreams.

Chapter 2

How It All Began

The next morning, I decided to pull out my money-related notes and files from years past. These money-related file folders had been stored in the bottom drawer of my desk for as long as I can remember. The folder that caught my attention was the tattered red folder. I wondered, *Why a red file?* A red folder peeked out from the drawer filled with manila file folders. It's probably the fact that red means stop. Stop! Stop spending. Stop mismanaging finances. Stop burying your head in the sand, so-to-speak. I reached for the red folder, knowing it was most likely the one containing information about the amounts of money I owed and to which agencies. I hesitated. Really hesitated. My moment of reckoning.

Nonetheless, I knew it was time. Time to get serious about managing money and time to create a plan- a pathway for success. Thinking of family… sisters, mom, nieces, nephews, brothers-in-law… I was determined to find a way to handle my finances. Family is, and always has been, important to me. I am blessed with a wonderful mom, two beautiful sisters (inside and out) and two brothers-in-law I consider brothers. Spending time with my nieces and nephews and creating memories I hoped would last a lifetime has been my greatest joy. My family has always been extremely supportive of my career as a teacher and professor, so I knew they were proud of me. However, I did not want to reach a point in my life, now or later, when I would face them with shame, guilt, or embarrassment because I had not handled money responsibly. Family nor friends were aware of my financial situation. You may understand. You may be struggling in silence. Or, you may be one who is completely open with others about your money-related decisions. Either way, the talk of money management, for most of us, is no fun at all!

Back to the tattered red folder. As I opened it, two small bags fell onto my lap. These bags contained pieces of credit cards. I opened the bags and took out the pieces. Some were stacked and held together with binder clips. Others were loose in the bag. Looking at these pieces, I decided to put them together as if they were pieces of a puzzle. As I knew would be the case, the pieces formed credit cards. But the *number* of credit cards! Not one. Not two. Not five or six. But, a total of nine credit cards. Nine!

Staring at these nine credit cards pieced together, emotions surfaced. A wide range of emotions. Did I look at these pieces of cards with regret? No. Well, sure, with some regret. But more importantly, I was mad. Mad at myself for having opened and used these cards. Cards from places I hardly remember visiting. I was frustrated. Frustrated not only with the number of and use of credit cards, but, also with myself for having so many notes and pages of budgeting attempts inside this tattered red folder. Yet, after all those efforts I was still so deeply in debt.

Looking through the pages of notes documenting credit card balances, I could see evidence of my attempt to create a plan for paying off debt, but the path was unclear. You may have done the same at some point in your life. Made notes about your financial state and outlined plans to tackle debt or created a spreadsheet on your computer to track spending, but to no avail. That effort was as far as I got.

Tattered Red Folder

Questions swirled in my head. *How had this started? When did I begin this journey toward debt accumulation?* I sat at my desk with the tattered red folder in hand and recalled the time after college graduation when my job search began.

****

Special Memory

The summer after I finished college and applied to Fulton County Schools in Atlanta, Georgia, I lived with my mom and little sister. To help prepare for interviews, my mom took me to a nice clothing store in the small town where we lived. I knew there was no extra money and it wasn't until later in life, much later, I truly knew how tough times were for our family, financially. But as we entered the store, my mom's face reflected such pride. Pride that her first of three daughters to finish college was preparing for her first job. Pride that I had become a teacher. There were teachers in her life who made a profound impact on her journey from a farm in northern Alabama to Washington D.C., where she began her first job after high school. Mom purchased a tailored black suit and two beautiful blouses for me to wear to interviews. Not only did I wear the suit to interviews, but also to PTA meetings, conferences, and special occasions... for many years. I wore that suit out! Each time I wore them I thought about the shopping trip and the loving look on my mom's face during the experience.

****

Thinking back, did I allow myself to connect emotionally with the purchase of clothes for interviews beyond that of creating the special memory of purchasing a suit for interviews- the sole purpose of the shopping trip? Instead, did I begin to equate expensive clothes with good feelings?

Back to how it all began. I remember receiving my first credit card. I had begun my first year of teaching with Fulton County Schools and was renting my first home, a duplex near the elementary school where I was hired to teach fourth grade. (Notice, lots of "firsts" during this time of my life.) This duplex was an old house, one that needed serious cleaning. But I was willing to scrub, clean, and scrub some more. I was so excited to have a "place" of my own. It was a house in an older part of the city with no amenities, lawn service, or nearby restaurants and shops. However, it was my home, a place to sleep and work as I prepared for my first classroom of students. My first job. The start to my life as a college graduate.

As I sat at my desk in my new condo with credit card pieces in hand, I continued thinking about the time of my first job and remembered I had also purchased a new car, a Chevy Monza. My car payment was in an amount comparable to the cost of rent. *At least, my car was clean! The duplex was old, but my car was new!*

Thinking back, once again, did I purchase a new car to compensate for an old duplex/home? Did I need a new car to feel good about my life? How could this be when I had secured a wonderful teaching job?

Furthermore, as a beginning teacher in a school with few resources, I "needed" to buy materials for my classroom. After all, I wanted the school year to be a terrific year for my students. I knew I wanted to make the year the best it could possibly be for these children, *my kids*. During my first month or two of teaching, the cost of groceries, utilities, and gas began to mount.

About that time, I received a gas card in the mail. (I had applied for it at the time of college graduation.) It came with a $500 credit limit. Upon receipt, I thought, *What great timing! This card could help with gas and if I needed a few things from inside the mini-mart, I could run in and use my card.* The phrase, "use my card," became my go-to. *Until next month, I can use my card,* seemed to be my approach for handling expenses when my paycheck ran out toward the end of the month.

This experience with my first credit card took place in 1979, the same year I began my career in teaching- a career I loved and treasured for 38 years and a career through which I carried credit card debt for more than three decades. Some years, the level of debt was more significant than others. From 2007-2016, my level of debt was at its highest; yet, my career had flourished and to the world's eyes- I was successful. It was mid-way through this time I created a plan, found my focus, and experienced what it truly means to live a debt-free life.

I wish for you, the reader, to take your first step toward debt-free living while reading this book. Now. Today. You may have been in debt for months, perhaps years, even decades, but you can do this. You just need to examine the real situation, consider the "pieces of the puzzle," and take a step toward your pathway for success. Let's work though this together.

****

When people believe their basic qualities can be developed, failures may still hurt, but failures don't define them. And if abilities can be expanded- if change and growth are possible- then there are still many paths to success.

Carol Dweck
Mindset

****

Chapter 3

You Know You Want To

I placed the tattered red folder on my desk and stood up from my chair. Walking across the room, I picked up my purse and opened my wallet. Yes, three credit cards remained in my wallet- two bank cards and one credit union card. In addition to the nine shredded cards in the bags, I had three others- *not* shredded! I pulled two credit cards from their designated slots in my wallet, walked back to my desk and removed a pair of scissors from the middle drawer. Yes, you guessed it. Snip! Crunch! I cut up the first of the two, the one with a $20,000 credit limit and then with another painstaking snip, I cut the second which held a credit limit of $7,000. I knew both were near their limits, anyway. (More about the credit union card later.) Can you imagine? Eleven credit cards! Perhaps you can. The number of cards you are juggling may not be eleven. Perhaps fewer. Perhaps more. Nevertheless, you want to stop. Just as the color, red, symbolized danger for me when looking at my tattered red folder, there was a desire to stop. Stop charging. Stop mismanaging finances. Stop ignoring a call to action. Stop living a debt-filled life!

Cutting the two cards and adding those pieces to the bag made it seem as if I wanted... really wanted... to bring an end to this mess of which I was deeply ashamed. You may feel the same. You know you have what it takes, yet you question yourself. Let me tell you. It can be done. You are *not* alone.

The bag of credit card pieces represented years of living in debt, as well as the challenges I faced while accumulating debt. Student loan debt. Car loan debt. Bank card debt. Furniture store debt. Clothing store credit card debt. Can you relate to any of these? You may be adding to this list as you read.

Based on my conversations with others in debt, there are two "schools of thought" regarding credit card debt. Some of you may be thinking it's easier to manage numerous credit cards as opposed to one or two because the payments due each month don't seem as large. Several payments. Smaller amounts on each. Or, you may be among those who have chosen to use one credit card with a hefty credit limit so you can "keep everything together" making it easier for you to manage. One payment. How many of us have read the credit card terms- the fine print? Do your eyes simply scan the statement for the "minimum due" and the date on which the payment is due, but avoid calculating interest rate accrual? So many of us do.

For the period, 2007-2010, copies of paystubs reflecting a good salary, combined with random notes about trying to pay off debt and manage money, reflected *some* effort on my part. It was clear. I had made attempts. I listed monthly expenses. Instead of thinking about a plan for tackling debt, I paid minimum amounts to leave as much money as possible for "other expenses" throughout the month. *After all, you never know what is going to arise during any given month.* You may be thinking the same. If you pay the minimum due, you have a better chance of making ends meet. (Think about the words used in this sentence alone. Minimum due. Chance. Making ends meet.) This was not the way I wanted to continue living- making ends meet. No! It had to stop.

In 2010, I read Suze Orman's book, *Women and Money*. I clearly remember the chapter, "No Shame, No Blame." In this chapter, Suze wrote about the burden of shame many women carry. She continued by writing, "You don't feel confident in your knowledge of how money works, so you hide behind the shame of it, deferring decisions to others or staying stuck in a pattern of inaction."

How true these words rang for me! Stuck. Stuck in a

pattern of inaction.

I was on my own. Regardless of past experiences and circumstances, I was on my own and blamed only myself. The shame was overwhelming, and it was burdensome. Was I alone? Were any of my friends struggling with debt? Do you wonder if you are alone? Do you sometimes think those around you seem to have it together and life seems manageable for them, financially speaking, and you are the only one with debt?

****

Special Memory

Years ago, when teaching fifth grade, I applied for a school district grant in the same academic year as I was working on my master's degree. (To this day, the original application is in one of my "Special Memories of Teaching" boxes in my home.) I wanted to create an interdisciplinary unit integrating social studies, economics, mathematics, and citizenship. (Ironically, the teaching of mathematics was my strongest content area.) This unit would actively involve all students in the development of a mini society. As part of our mini society, I worked with my students to create a currency system so a mini-economy program could be incorporated allowing students to apply for classroom jobs, earn a salary, pay taxes, pay rent (for their classroom crate/locker), make decisions about saving and spending, and maintain careful record-keeping sheets to reflect deposits and withdrawals from their personal accounts. Each student had an envelope (wallet) housed in his/her desk. All students worked together to earn classroom bonuses to encourage collaboration and group effort throughout the pay periods. How fun it was to teach decimals and percent as students used their individual record-keeping sheets for problem solving! Real world application made the study of mathematics and financial literacy meaningful. Students enjoyed it. The class worked collaboratively. We covered content. They developed life skills. It was a wonderful experience! I continued incorporating the mini economy into my teaching during subsequent years because the novelty of such a program in the elementary school classroom never became "old" and the skills taught were always applicable to "real life."

While teaching financial literacy in this way, I had the pleasure of listening to young students talk about the impact of taxes on earnings, cost of rent, difficult decisions regarding expenses related to insurance and proposed "life scenarios" included in content-related activities at the end of each week. Some students displayed enthusiasm when watching their savings accounts grow while others made decisions to spend.

Clearly, I recall one student who saved every dollar earned. Others spent money during Market Day, Friday Auctions, and School Store. This student paid rent, taxes, insurance, and covered expenses incurred through "life scenarios" but spent nothing more. He was a "saver." I remember the look on students' faces when, at the end of the school year, he had his savings in hand... in cash. What a profound impact it had on our class!

At the time I was making final edits to this book, I had the pleasure of spending time with several of my previous students. Now, thirteen years later, these young professionals speak about the life skills learned through the mini-economy program taught during math and social studies. Who knew I would have the opportunity to see some of the students about whom I had written a special memory to share with my readers? Who knew I would be presented the opportunity to have a face-to-face conversation with the young man who saved his earnings during his fifth-grade mini economy classroom experience? He told me he remembered thinking, "Now what will I do with all this cash?" Today, as an adult, he continues to save... for a house.

****

Now… how crazy was this! A success at school teaching financial literacy to my fifth-grade students, yet I was not "practicing what I preached" at home with *my own* personal finances. Really? How could this be?

Some of you may relate to this scenario. You may be single or married. A parent, aunt, uncle, grandparent or godparent. A student or working professional. Yet, you go home to a "red folder," so- to- speak, and struggle with managing finances. It happens. You are **not** alone.

Money, more specifically, debt, is not a topic people often discuss. There *are* others struggling with debt. There *are* others with little or no knowledge of budgeting. There *are* successful professionals who seem to have it all together, yet in the area of finances, simply do not. It is possible to be fully committed to doing excellent work yet be "off task" in the area of finances. I first came to this realization when reading *Women and Money* written by Suze Orman. It occurred to me. I am *not* alone. I will forever be thankful for Suze's dedication to helping women in the area of finances. On more than one occasion, I have heard Suze say, "If you are going down the street the wrong way, remember, God permits U-turns."

When I am passionate about an area of life, such as faith, family, friends or teaching, I give myself wholeheartedly. I read, take classes, spend time with people and am always interested in self-improvement. Becoming a better teacher, professor, daughter, sister, aunt, friend, leader, and volunteer has always been in the forefront of my mind as I read, reflect, and continually work to make positive changes in these roles of which I am most proud. *Why, though, had I not applied these same efforts to managing finances?*

You may be passionate about certain areas of your life. You may be reading books about caring for a newborn or dealing with teenagers' moods. It could be you are involved in professional development by reading articles and listening to podcasts on topics related to effective leadership, entrepreneurship, or the improvement of work-related skills. You may be interested in health and fitness, so you spend a great deal of time on the tennis court, running, working out or cooking well-balanced meals. But at what level have you pursued personal growth in the area of finances?

With such questions as these running through my mind, I thought, *Enough with this pattern of inaction*! It was time to respond to a call to action.

I had heard of Dave Ramsey's Financial Peace University classes, often referred to as FPU. Around our city, these classes were offered in churches. I knew I could research the area in which I lived and, hopefully, sign up online. However, would I have the nerve to walk into a church and make my way to a class about financial peace… as a participant with very little understanding of what it meant to manage finances? I knew I wanted to do so. For me, it was that deep-down feeling of knowing I wanted those I love and care for, those who are proud of the work I do in education, to see I could be responsible in this area of life as well. (The thing is, at the time of researching FPU offerings, no one knew I was struggling with debt, so no one knew this was my area of shame.) But, thinking long-term, I wanted to be in a position so that all areas of life I lived to the very best of my ability. I always believed any job worth doing is worth doing with excellence. *This belief should be no different for the job I do managing money*, I decided.

That was it. That was the thinking behind my decision to work toward becoming financially free. I made the decision and researched a broad area around my zip code, hoping to find a class offered at a small church located miles away. This way, I could "slip into class" without anyone's recognizing me, take the class and see if it would help me get started. (Do I sound like a twelve-year-old, or what?)   What held me back?   Shame. Embarrassment. The emotions often associated with debt. Need I say more? Can you relate?

Stay with me and continue reading. You can do this. The antidote to fear is action. Take another step. Turn the page. You've got this!

Chapter 4

The Fearless Leap

****

I have learned over the years that when one's mind is made up, this diminishes fear; knowing what must be done does away with fear.
-Rosa Parks
****

After searching, I found it. I found a church offering Dave Ramsey's Financial Peace University (FPU). Now the question was, did I have the nerve to move forward, to take that step? Why was the decision so difficult? I remember applying to grad school and being nervous about the first night of class. I remember working through the process of writing a dissertation for my doctorate. Why is facing the truth about my management of finances and seeking help so difficult? Do you feel this way? Are you hesitant to take that first step, yourself? If so, for what reason? We all read about success stories in our newsfeeds. News articles highlight people getting out of debt or couples saving extraordinary amounts of money in a short period of time. Podcasts address the topic of building wealth. It's out there. Information about managing finances is available to us. But *we* must take the leap.

However, for many of us the reasons for ignoring calls of action to start the journey toward a debt-free life run deep. We may consider ourselves financially illiterate, lack knowledge about budgeting, or have little or no understanding of cash flow patterns.

Well, no more. No more dreaming about what it would be

like to be free of debt. No more files filled with notes and written attempts for budgeting, yet little or no follow-up. No more. Instead, I decided to face my fear- fear of being judged, fear of disappointing colleagues if they learned of this "weak area" of my life, and fear of failure.

I made the decision to take the course, Financial Peace University (FPU), at a small church north of the city where I lived. I did it! I registered for the course. On the first evening of class, I walked into the church alone and navigated my way to the room where the class met. When I walked in, I was relieved to see I did not recognize anyone. A married couple served as co-leaders and introduced themselves.   They were welcoming and kind. Nonthreatening.   As I looked around the room, I noticed a combination of couples and single people. Within a short period of time that first evening, I began to take comfort in the fact that I was not alone in my struggles. Furthermore, I believed enrolling in the class was the right decision, the right first step.

Included in the registration fee was a copy of Dave Ramsey's book, *The Total Money Makeover*, and a workbook. Instruction videos were shown at the beginning of each weekly class.   In the videos, Dave Ramsey talked about steps for managing money, referred to as Baby Steps. He discussed the importance of a $1,000 emergency fund and a zero-based budget, neither of which I had. A zero-based budget, as explained by Dave Ramsey, is to make income minus the outgo equal zero. I was intrigued by the budgeting process and used the record-keeping sheet included in the workbook.   This sheet outlined recommended percentages of income for categories of expenses, including, but not limited to housing, food, transportation, insurance, clothing, and toiletries. Never had I listed expenses in such a detailed way. For most years of my life, I spent money until it was gone, then struggled or used a credit card toward the end of the month. But, tracking spending and designating specific amounts of income for these categories did make sense to me.

Working through this part of FPU, the establishment of a $1,000 emergency fund and creation of a budget, seemed to take longer for me than most. Each time I designated an amount of money for a category, I found the need to adjust. The leaders of the class explained this adjustment was part of the process. As I sat near the back of the room so I would not have to "share" during discussions, I thought about ways I could adjust my spending. I am a "deep thinker" and, as I said earlier, I read and reflect on any topic that interests me. Furthermore, it is important for me to have time to process information, then determine the best approach to take when applying what I learned. While spending time working on my budget, the class continued to move on to sessions about debt snowball, mortgages, and insurance.

When we reached the session on whole life vs term life insurance, I was overwhelmed. All I could think about was the amount of debt for which I was responsible. In class, we had moved on to important life decisions, such as insurance and building wealth, but I was stuck working on a budget and trying to account for every dollar. I embraced the idea of using cash for weekly expenses and, for the past few weeks, carried envelopes for cash in my purse. It was a challenge for me to absorb the content presented in class when I had so much on my mind regarding budgeting and paying off debt. Still, I attended the sessions and continued listening and taking notes.

Let me interject a comment. Creating a budget through FPU using the worksheet, "Monthly Cash Flow Plan," assisted with my start to getting out of debt. I've heard some people say a budget isn't needed; instead, be wise with spending. This strategy may work for those who learned to manage money at an early age or married someone who embraced the principles of money management; however, as a grown adult trying to find a stepping stone for that first step toward debt-free living following decades of living with debt, a budget was crucial. I will forever be appreciative of Dave Ramsey's Monthly Cash Flow Plan worksheet. I referenced this sheet when creating a budget format that worked for me.

I understood and recognized the value of creating and following a budget. It was now time to become as passionate about managing money and paying off debt as I was about teaching. What about you? Is it time? It seems so. You are still reading this book and thinking about your desire to begin your journey toward a debt-free life. You can do it. You can. The first step is the hardest. But before long, your first step turns into another, then another. Stick with me. Let's do this!

Chapter 5

Facing the Truth

****

It takes as much energy to wish as it does to plan.
-Eleanor Roosevelt

****

Learning to budget takes time. Sticking to a budget takes discipline. Planning to follow a budget sets you on your pathway for success. It can be done. If I can do it, so can you!

In addition to budgeting, I knew I had to take a deep dive into my debt. Exactly how much did I owe? To whom? When were payments due? What was the minimum payment due for each? These were questions I could answer, for the most part. After all, I had been opening the bills, making minimum payments, at least, and creating outlines for possible ways to pay off debt. When beginning the FPU classes, I had a rough estimate of the amount of money I owed and shared it with the co-leaders. I knew, though, I needed to take a thorough, more accurate account of the money I owed, so I braced myself.

I believed I could develop the discipline needed to continue following the budget I created. As challenging as it was, I had crossed that first hurdle and taken the step to find support and encouragement. Now, though, it was time to face the truth about debt: "grand" total amount owed. I had to know this to effectively create a strategy for paying my debts and continue moving down a path toward debt-free living.

21

The files and notes I planned to review would provide evidence of the truth I must face. My tattered red folder was filled with figures reflecting income and budgeting sheets created during 2010-2012, including outlines of ideas and strategies for paying off different debts, timelines, and notes to self- notes of encouragement for paying off debt. The mark X was written over many of the notes as if to reflect the lack of success putting the ideas into motion. I searched through papers looking for a chart of amounts owed to each company and agency. There was no such chart. *Had this task been too challenging to complete? Was it the fear of facing the truth about the total amount owed? Was this the reason such a chart did not exist?* You may understand what I am saying. I had made attempts to get a handle on my finances, but I had not created a plan.

A sense of dread poured over me. *Where do I begin?* It was the end of 2012. Debts seem more manageable when considered individually. However, a grand total seemed too overwhelming to ponder. After all, when debt-related information is written, when you see it on paper, it becomes real. Real painful, that is.

It was obvious. Facing the truth, the whole truth, about finances *had* to be the next step. With this, I knew a wide array of emotions would surface. Shame. Guilt. Disappointment. Embarrassment. Need I go on?

Such emotions are not linked to mathematical abilities. Emotions linked to debt are personal. For each of you reading this book, different emotions may surface as you relate to parts, or all, of my story.

When writing this book, with the intention of reaching out to those who are stuck and unsure of the best way to begin managing finances responsibly, I thought about those who are frozen for whatever reason. Initially, in my journey, I thought "facing the truth" was simply facing the truth about the total amount of money owed then creating a plan to pay off all debts. A deep dive into the "truth," however, led me to the identification of the reasons I mismanaged money.

Once again, the answer was fear. Fear of not spending money on things or experiences to make myself or others feel better. Fear of being without. Fear of not purchasing items to make myself or others experience happiness. Fear of not trying to make "everything ok" for those I love. Can you relate to such thoughts as these? You are not alone. Keep reading. Stay with me. In the chapter, "Debt is Personal," we will continue exploring this concept.

Puzzling to me when facing the truth about the total amount of debt I owed was the fact that I liked to plan. I am a planner. Throughout my adult life, I have been goal-oriented, a detailed planner, and one who outlines necessary steps to reach each goal. Such planning has been an integral part of my career throughout years of teaching elementary, middle and high school levels, then transitioning to the college classroom to work with future teachers and loving each step of the way. Yet, there was no evidence of this "planner" side of me in the tattered red folder which housed the notes related to my management of money throughout past decades.

You may be able to relate to this scenario. I must emphasize this point again. Perhaps you handle certain areas of life beautifully, such as parenting, marriage, work, personal health, managing your home, or volunteering, yet your finances are out of order. You get it. You understand how this *can* happen. It is possible for a loving mother, hard-working father, dedicated teacher, motivated entrepreneur, or serious student, to be struggling with debt- young or mature in years. You are **not** alone.

Enough moving through this area of life blindly and irresponsibly! I knew it was time to create a pathway for success. I had reached the point when I was no longer going to avoid a call to action. I was ready.

Thoughts may be racing through your mind. You may be somewhat satisfied with your ability to pay bills, even though you carry a hefty amount of debt. Reading this book, though, indicates your desire for moving beyond that point. You are ready to do something about your dismal financial state and move toward a sense of relief. Living a debt-free life is appealing. You know you can do this.

Your debt may be personal and private. Perhaps, you have told no one. You may be too embarrassed to share your situation with family members or friends. I understand. No one knew my plight. No one. You are not alone. There are others around you with the same dream of living a debt-free life. Wake up. You can do this.

Here it is. Taped to my red folder is a post-it with figures reflecting my total debt, as it stood in 2012 when I decided to take hold of my finances and continue the journey toward debt-free living.

The Start to my "Facing the Truth Chart"

In early 2013, my credit card debt totaled $49,300. My student loan debt stood at $76,800, and my car loan balance was $17,340. As you can see, the total amount exceeded $140,000. My mortgage was not included in this amount.

Still, though, I had not itemized. I had not listed each credit card company, agency, or organization I still owed money, including the balance of each, nor had I calculated the "grand" total. Rifling through papers and documents in my tattered red folder, I did just this. I created a chart (see below) and filled in the information, painful as it was. I needed to *face the truth* about my debt. Writing this information using pen and paper, holding the chart in my hands, and staring at the "grand" total served as a dramatic wake-up call.

C Marie's "Facing the Truth" Chart

Agency	Balance Owed
Student Loan	$76,800
Car Loan	$17, 340
CC #1	$18,559
CC #2	$ 6,714
CC #3	$ 9,407
CC #4	$ 1,193
Credit Union Loan #1	$ 450
Credit Union Loan #2	$ 4,711
Bank Line of Credit	$ 8,266

"**Grand**" Total = $143,440 (excluding mortgage)

There is nothing "grand" about debt!

I entered the information into my computer for easy access to print and put before me as I moved forward. I took another step and created a more detailed document to include agencies, total amount owed to each, minimum due each month, and interest rate paid to each.

There is something about the written word, so-to-speak. When information is in front of you, in black and white, it is real. No more pretending *it* doesn't exist. No more tucking *it* away in the back of a desk drawer. By this point, I was following a budget and applying every dollar I saved from adjusting poor spending habits. Now, "facing the truth" about the debt I owed, combined with my decision to budget the money I earned, resulted in a strong desire to move forward along the path I was creating. I had a designated drawer of my desk that held my budget sheet for the month, notes written on my budget sheet to reflect positive habits I was developing, and my "Facing the Truth Chart." I reviewed these every day. And by, review, I mean I consistently reviewed my finances every day. Money spent was recorded on my budget sheet- daily. I had receipts for all expenses and recorded the amounts on my budget sheet. As I adjusted spending habits and saved, even as little as one dollar, I applied that amount to the debt I owed.

As I recorded the money I applied toward debt, I found I wanted to "speed up the process," so I started working part-time on Saturdays in an interior design shop. I enjoyed the work and my schedule was such that my hours did not interfere with my job at the university. For those of you in retail, you understand what it is like standing on the sales floor for a full eight hours. When you finish your day, you're too tired to go out to eat and spend money! Seriously, though, I share this with you because you may find you need more money and a second job, be it on weekends, evenings, or online.

By now, I had a focus. I wanted to continue down this path. As I had always done, put forth my best effort teaching at the university. I chose to teach summer classes and assume the role of program coordinator for two reasons; I enjoyed teaching and I earned additional income. I chose to continue working on Saturdays at the interior design shop. All income beyond the necessities outlined in my monthly budget was applied toward debt and recorded on my "Facing the Truth Chart."

As I tried to organize my budget sheets, monthly bank statements, credit card statements, and receipts, I found the task to be somewhat overwhelming. As you spend time assembling your notes and files as you create your budget and "Facing the

Truth Chart," you may be thinking, "Is this what life is going to be like?   Commitment to a budget and strict spending habits? Chipping away at debt little by little? Do I *really* keep this up for months... years?"

Yes! That is exactly what you do. Keep it up! You can do it!

Turn the page. You will find you can take the next step in a matter of minutes. You've got this!

Chapter 6

Organization

****

I can wrestle with something for a long time, but once I make up my mind, I'm all in.

-Joanna Gaines
The Magnolia Story

****

The word, organization, holds different meanings for different people. For some of you, the thought of moving to a new office and "setting up" or purchasing school supplies to begin a new year thrills you. You enjoy the challenge of finding new ways to organize your files, desk, office, home or apartment. Others of you may freeze, holding your breath for a second as you envision the piles of papers and documents inhabiting areas of your office or home. Or, yet, a quick look inside your purse or laptop bag reveals a wad of crumpled receipts, bills to be paid or other documents.

It may be the idea of connecting the "puzzle pieces," finances and organization, is enough to hold you back from continuing your journey toward debt-free living. The role organization plays in *Wake Up to the Dream of a Debt-Free Life* is simply that of an organized space for storing and managing your budget-related documents. (Some of you may be thinking, "C Marie, there is nothing simple about getting organized!")

Your organization style for your journey-to-be-debt-free documents may be that of paper files and folders or electronic.

Your choice. Let's call this area your "I Can Do This" space. If you are using a computer, as opposed to paper files and folders, call it your "I Can Do This" desktop folder.

My personal "I Can Do This" space has been the bottom left drawer of my dad's desk. My dad, a wonderfully kind man, passed away soon after I graduated from Berry College. This special seven-drawer desk belonged to him and was given to me following college graduation. It became a part of my home...my 14 residences... from 1979-2019. Inside the drawer designated as my "I Can Do This" space, I housed my tattered red folder, budget sheets, bills (those not sent and paid electronically), and my "Facing the Truth Chart" of debts I owed.

In the narrow middle drawer, just below the top of the desk, I wrote a note of encouragement to myself in 2013, *Give, Save, Live off the Rest. Be debt-free by 2020. You can do it!* Each time I opened the drawer, there it was, front and center!

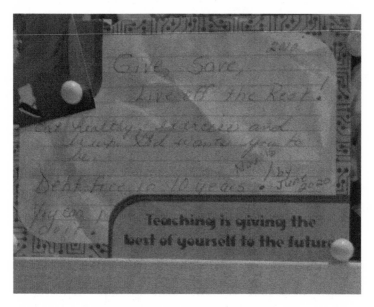

Give, Save, Live off the Rest!

My "I Can Do This" space included a second drawer that contained a devotional book, journals, notes from Sunday messages, and my Bible.

These three drawers served as my "I Can Do This" space throughout my journey to a debt-free life. Your home, apartment, or dorm may be more limited in space. You may have a crate or file box serving as your "I Can Do This" space or it could be you have an entire office with unlimited drawer and cabinet space. Perhaps you have chosen to maintain all documents and files on your laptop. Whatever works for you. Again, debt is personal. Your journey is unique. Each step of the way may be like others yet vary based on your life circumstance. That's the beauty of a journey. It's individual, personal, and unique. Go ahead. Designate a space and consider naming it your "I Can Do This." Because... you *can* do this! You *can* continue your journey toward a debt-free life! Keep going! Your time is now!

Chapter 7

Debt is Personal

****

Whatever your present situation, I assure you that you are not your habits. You can replace old patterns of self-defeating behavior with new patterns, new habits of effectiveness, happiness, and trust-based relationships.

-Stephen R. Covey
The 7 Habits of Highly Effective People
****

When facing the truth about debt, you will find the truth extends beyond the list of companies, agencies, and persons to whom you owe money. The truth extends beyond the mathematics involved in developing a budget or charting a plan for tackling debt. There are reasons for debt, for mismanagement of money.

Each of our paths toward becoming free of debt may look different, as the hurdles we encounter or create for ourselves vary. Hurdles may include, but are not limited to, lack of budgeting, poor spending habits developed over a time, job changes, relationships, or need for organization.

But, before we go any further, take a few moments to think about your debt and the possible reasons associated with it. It may be helpful to consider the questions below. Go ahead. Make notes in the margins of this book or place post-it notes on the pages. If you are one who journals, you may want to record your thoughts in your journal. This is important. Consider the following:

- When reviewing your list of debts (student loan debt, credit card debt, car loan debt, personal loan debt, etc.), which is largest? Does your list reflect what is most important to you?
- Have you pulled a credit card statement, online or hard copy, only to be shocked by the total amount charged during the statement period and asked yourself, "How did it add up to such a large amount? Each charge seemed small, but when added together the sum seems ridiculously high." In which categories did you find your greatest expenses? After careful consideration, do your best to categorize these charges into necessary and unnecessary purchases.
- Following a divorce or the death of a spouse, you try to manage finances on your own. If so, for what amount of time have you been paying the bills? Have you created a record-keeping system for managing finances? If so, has it worked or worked only for a time?
- After years of being single, are you newly married and trying to openly manage finances with your husband or wife? What debt did you bring into the marriage?
- Are you a single mom raising children and doing your best to provide for them, including, but not limited to clothing, activities, and special events? Write a few notes about monthly spending in these areas.
- Do you express your love and care for others through gift giving? If someone in your life

appears sad, tired, or in need of encouragement, do you enjoy purchasing items you believe will help him or her feel better?

- Is retail therapy part of your life? That new outfit you just had to have for the special event or outing... was it worth it? Even though it seemed important at the time, did you later question whether you needed to have made that purchase?

- Is the newest model of phone, style of handbag, golf course, weekend activities, model of automobile or vacation destination important to you? Are you "caught up" in it all? If so, how has this need for the latest gadget or fashion item affected your spending in recent years?

The purpose of this list of questions is to activate thoughts about spending. *Your* spending. It is important to be cognizant of your thoughts. Thoughts lead to actions. Through this process, we can develop new habits to support our efforts in the journey to become free of debt.

What the purpose of this exercise is *not* is to think about your life and compare it to others. Instead, make note of your thoughts about spending and think about your notes. Self-reflection. Deep reflection. Think about what you are thinking. I am serious. Reflect on your thoughts about spending. When do you spend money? On the way home from work when you are tired? During the weekend when you are lonely? At times when you want to please someone or make another feel better? When you want to feel better about yourself? Is the stress of managing finances so difficult, you feel better when you shop... and then you don't?

Debt is personal. Each person has accumulated debt for reasons of his or her own. Comparing your life to that of a family member, friend, neighbor or coworker can steer you off course. When making such comparisons you may think others have it easier than you. For example, as a single person, you may have read the list of questions and spent time thinking about ways the journey toward becoming free of debt would be easier if you had a spouse with whom to share expenses. If you are married, you may be thinking how easy it must be for singles seemingly caring for only themselves. Parents, you may be thinking how things must be different for a mom with *no* children at home. But, stop. Comparison gets us nowhere. None of us knows the complete circumstances of others' lives. Each person deals with her own set of struggles, just as you do. Some may be lonely. Others need alone time. Some may be wishing for companionship. Others may be smothered by the people around them. Some may be running a tight schedule rushing from one child's sporting event to another, while others may wish for that very opportunity. Some may be young and have years ahead for paying debt and saving for the future, while others of you may be starting this journey at a mature age. Rather than comparing yourself to others, think about *your* goal- to become free of debt while living a full life.

Debt Is Emotional

As stated in the chapter, "How It All Began," it was late 2012 after spending the first night in my new loft condo when I made the decision to assemble my money-related notes and files from years past. Debt generates emotions. I can certainly attest to this! Handling these emotions about my financial state, I believe, is what led to my success in becoming free of debt. Was I angry? Yes, but not with others. Shifting blame or projecting anger toward others was not the answer. Thinking about the emotion, what led to it, and what could be done about the situation is the action I took. If I wanted to become free of debt, I had to assume responsibility for the process.

Think about the emotions associated with your financial state. For example, I was angry when I reviewed my notes and files. You may recall I had nine credit cards. I did cut them into pieces, drop the pieces into a plastic bag, and staple the bag to my red, finance-related file folder. Evidence existed I once had plans for tackling debt. Nonetheless, I was angry. Angry at myself for the "charging" these credit cards pieces represented in past years-past decades. Now, I was left holding a bag of credit card pieces no longer used yet I continued to make payments on the balance each held. In my mind, the amount of interest I had paid and continued to pay most likely funded several floors of a high-rise bank building! And, nice leather furniture to boot! And, coffee and donuts for all employees every morning of the year! And... need I go on? You get what I am saying! You, too, may believe the amount of credit card interest you have paid contributed to the growth of large banks.

It's tempting, I know, to take that anger, grab a bag of M&Ms, sit and complain about high interest rates, blame others for expenses, or accuse credit card companies of clever marketing strategies leading to the opening of accounts. Instead, considering your emotions and redirect them to positive thoughts about paying your debts. Let me continue with my example. Yes, I was angry when I looked at my pieces of credit cards and thought about the high balances I carried, the large amount of interest paid, and the fact that I could hardly remember what was purchased to lead to such a significant amount of debt. Consider this question: *Based on what you know about your finances, what two actions or habits contributed unnecessarily to your level of debt?* For me, the response to that question sparked anger. Anger with myself. Two habits I needed to address at the time included strolling through superstores and eating out. I had developed a habit of strolling through a superstore with the intent of purchasing laundry soap and paper towels but somehow ending up in the kitchen and bath or new arrivals aisles. Perusing these sections of the store often resulted in unnecessary purchases. Seeing a candle with a scent I simply "had to have" for the kitchen. While I was at it, why shouldn't I pick one up for a friend or family member? The sportswear I was drawn to would most likely result in additional trips to the gym or trails for walking, right? Are you with me? Perhaps your thoughts include comments such as, "The clearance aisle is loaded with items. I can't afford *not* to pick up a few things for the kids." Things you didn't know you "needed." Are you with me?

Then, as many of you may know, there is that feeling of reaching check-out counter, listening to the sound of the computer beep as each item is scanned, then waiting for the total cost... hoping it is less than... drumroll, please... $____! Well, you understand what I am saying. The cost of items can add up so quickly, especially when there is lack of intention when shopping.

During a Sunday message, I remember hearing my pastor share the concept, awareness fuels discontentment. Until you "see" it, you don't know you "need" it. Pending walking into the superstore for the laundry detergent, I was unaware of the items I "needed" from the aisles pulling at me from all directions.

I share this with you because it was important for *me* to think about my emotions associated with the truth about debt. Debt is emotional. Debt is personal. Each of our circumstances may look different, but bottom line, we need to learn- we *want* to learn- to manage our money responsibly and eliminate the habits preventing us from doing so.

The second of two habits I identified as being unnecessary in my life was the habit of eating out, a habit which can be expensive even though the restaurants chosen may be categorized as fast food or casual dining. Many of us have fallen into this habit and the reasons for eating out may be justified, at least in our minds. For instance, if you are single, eating out may be a way for you to be around other people. If you are a parent, you may find it easier to eat out or pick up food from a drive-thru on your way home from work. Perhaps, you had a difficult day and feel the need to "treat" yourself to a meal.

After serious thought, my anger turned to frustration, then to disappointment. Disappointment in myself. Disappointment in my mismanagement of money in this way. You may know all too well how quickly expenses add up when eating out and visiting drive-thru windows. For me, it was the idea of going home, cooking, and eating alone. I would have rather worked long hours than sit at home during "dinner hour" and eat alone. Sure, I could have met family and/or friends, but not daily. For you, the thought of an empty house after years of it filled with a spouse, children or roommates, you find you are adjusting to a different living environment.

I carefully considered my emotions... the frustration... turned disappointment and decided to adjust my habits. Commitment to paying off debt would require changes. I knew that to be true. Over time, I became more and more interested in healthy eating and read articles and books about eating clean. The following year I read the book, *Grain Brain* by David Perlmutter, MD. Giving more serious thought to my eating habits, I made decisions to purchase certain food items at the grocery and stay away from processed foods in the house. Don't get me wrong. When looking in my frig, you would often find a bag of chocolate with almond and toffee bars or chocolate mint treats. After all, I *needed* them to offer family and friends when they came to visit! Seriously, though, I made changes to eating habits resulting in a healthier me. And, the money spent on eating out as often was no longer slipping through my fingers.

My point is this. Choice. I *chose* to identify my emotions related to debt. I *chose* to give careful thought to the emotions. I *chose* to reflect on my emotions. The emotion, anger, was the first I experienced and addressed. After careful thought, I realized what I believed to be anger was frustration and disappointment, in disguise.

Instead of giving up the idea of ever becoming free of debt, I addressed the emotions and turned them into positive thoughts, actions, and habits. First, shopping in superstores vs. making a list of grocery items and cleaning products to take into a specific store for a specific purpose. Extra (unnecessary) purchases were no longer made. Second, eating out vs. healthy eating. Healthier eating became my new habit. Eating out was set aside for special occasions.

****

Special Memory

As I have shared with you, I enjoy spending time with my nieces and nephew. During the time I chose to cut back on eating out, I saved the special occasions for days I would see them. I usually picked them up and drove. Waiting for them in the car was a small bag containing several pieces of paper. On each piece, I had written the name of a restaurant. One of the kids would "draw" a name from the bag and decide if the restaurant appealed to them. If so, that's where we went. This gave them choices and it was fun for me because I could list restaurants we enjoyed, but also within budget.

****

Much of the reason I tried to make eating out a special "outing" was because both of my sisters always cooked what I call, real meals, for their families. I have always admired this about them. Planning, preparing, and serving family meals during which time they sat and talked with their husbands and children every evening.

Eating out became special, not ordinary. Within budget. Not charged. Hence, a positive result stemming from careful thought about my emotions associated with debt. New results. New habits. Taking steps along my pathway for success! Stick with me. It only gets better!

Another emotion I experienced when reviewing my money-related notes and files was that of embarrassment. As I poured over page after page of written notes reflecting attempts to manage money, I could see there were ways in which I had mismanaged money simply by lack of attention to detail. How could this be? Seriously? Following decades of teaching, careful lesson planning, hours of grading and providing detailed, meaningful feedback to students, as well as maintaining highly organized files, spreadsheets, and gradebooks, how could I have failed to apply such skills to my own personal finances?

How embarrassing this would be if anyone was aware of the way I managed my salary! Or would it be? I wondered if there was enough organized record-keeping for anyone to see how my money was spent. Why had I not created a plan for my money? Why had I not managed my income responsibly month to month and year to year? I know the answer. I never learned. I never attempted to learn. I never made this a priority. College degree? Check. Grad school? Check. Learning to become a more effective teacher and improve instructional strategies? Check. Attempting the study of financial literacy? Not even close! Financial literacy had not been part of my education at any level, nor had it been part of my pursuit of an education, post-graduate.

As I made the commitment to learn about budgeting, as well as explore strategies for tackling debt, I found myself becoming as excited about learning as I had when working on postgraduate degrees for teachers.

Chapter 8

Taking That First Step

One day, in retrospect, the years of struggle will strike you as the most beautiful.

-Sigmund Freud

Now is the time to construct your pathway for success.

In his book, *Better Than Good,* Zig Ziglar emphasized the importance of getting started. He reminded us of the words of the old Testament psalmist, "Thy word is a lamp to my feet and a light to my path" (Psalm 119:105). As Ziglar pointed out, lamps were not as we know them today. Lamps were small clay objects containing oil and a wick that produced light comparable to that of a candle. Think about the amount of light these lamps provided those who carried them. Simply enough to allow them to make their way one step at a time. This is what you can do when making the decision to become free of debt. Take a step. One step at a time- out of obscurity and into the light.

Chapter 9

Hope, Faith & Love

Faith, hope, and love. These three powerful, descriptive words, written or spoken in any order, are the most meaningful in my life.

At the onset of my journey toward becoming free of debt, I thought of these three words in terms of this scripture: "But now abide faith, hope and love, these three; but the greatest of these is love "(I Corinthians 13:13 New American Standard). This is a verse I memorized at an early age and later heard during wedding ceremonies. During my journey, however, each of these three words grew in significance. The "puzzle piece," Hope, Faith and Love, serves as the most influential in my journey. Certainly, the "puzzle piece," Finances, is prominent, but is not the foundation for my company, Puzzle Pieces to Pathway, LLC.

I hope to share with you both my journey toward becoming financially free and my unexpected faith journey leading to a debt-free life. For me, the two are intertwined and, based on my experience, there is no separating the two. For you, the reader, it is my intent to share with you the many life-enriching outcomes of the journey toward becoming free of debt.

Hope

When buried in debt, I admit embracing these three concepts, hope, faith and love, presented challenges for me. Let me explain. As you may remember reading in the chapter, "Facing the Truth," I had accumulated $143,440 in debt, excluding my mortgage. At that point, the word, *hope*, did not seem strong enough to reflect my thoughts about becoming free of debt. The reason? I was placing hope in myself. At my age. In my 50s. "Hoping" to get out of debt.

Allow me to fast forward a moment and share a memory to better explain the "puzzle piece," Hope, Faith & Love.

****

Special Memory

I clearly recall the month and year I became free of debt: November 2016. Free from the burden of debt in the amount of $143,440, excluding my mortgage. Free from student loan debt. Free from credit card debt. Free from car loan debt. Free from bank loan debt. Free.

Months prior to the event, I purchased a ticket to the 2016 Smart Conference to be held at North Point Community Church in Alpharetta, GA. I had purchased my ticket on March 26, 2016, (months in advance), with the goal of making my final debt-related payment before the event. The thought of attending this conference, led by Dave Ramsey and Rachel Cruze, generated emotions I could not put into words. I wanted to walk into the building knowing I had accomplished the challenge of becoming free of debt, sit and listen to the presenters... without feelings of

shame and guilt because I had mismanaged money for most...
most all... of my life. I wanted to cheer, not shed tears. I wanted
to applaud in support of those working to become free of debt. I
wanted to celebrate with a group striving to be better managers
of money. I wanted to sit among the attendees at North Point
Community Church.

Even though I imagined there would be tears as presenters
spoke, these tears would include tears of joy. Tears of joy
dumping student loan debt, credit card debt, personal loan debt,
bank line of credit debt, and car loan debt! I didn't know if I would
be proud to be seen by others or if old feelings of shame,
embarrassment, and guilt would prompt the thought: **I hope no**
one sees me!

****

The Smart Conference 2016 Event Guide is a booklet I
have saved and stored with my budget-related books and notes.
To me, it is a reminder of success I experienced following hurdles,
failures, and "get-back-up" moments along my pathway toward
becoming free of debt. I made notes in my event guide during
speaker presentations, and I recall Dave Ramsey's making a point
that success is stumbling from failure to failure with no loss of
enthusiasm. I thought about it. Not only was I enthusiastic
throughout my journey- enthusiastic about paying my debts, of
course, but also enthusiastic about what I believe to be life-
enriching outcomes.

Rolling into December (my favorite time of year), I greeted
the Christmas season free of debt. In years past, I had budgeted
monthly to save for Christmas gifts. December 2016 was the first
month I adjusted my budget to reflect this new debt-free life.
Adhering to a budget during the Christmas season took discipline,

not only for financial reasons, but also for reasons associated with my emotions. I love giving during the Christmas season. I love surprising family and friends. Who doesn't, right? Cutting back was tough. Really tough.

I remember giving great thought to giving, not just the giving of money, but the giving of time, resources, and talent. A sense of clarity washed over me. I thought, *If I had struggled with debt, I imagine there are others facing this same challenge. Many may be thinking there is no hope.* At that moment, my heart broke. I wondered how I could help others. I understand what this struggle means. I do.

Throughout the month of December, I spent a great deal of time thinking about my journey during the previous five years. I believe there is much more to the journey of becoming free of debt than simply working with money. I think there is a psychological adjustment to eliminating poor spending habits and developing positive habits leading to a debt-free life. Yes, it is difficult adjusting to a lesser amount of spending. Yes, it is difficult, to say the least, when you want to buy gifts for family and friends- those you love- but you've had to cut back on what you can do. However, was this "budget-aware" Christmas less than the extraordinary time of year it had always been? Absolutely not. I thought about what I referred to earlier in this section: life enriching outcomes of the journey.

Perhaps I could find a way to help others in debt take the first step toward a debt-free life and find a pathway for success, I thought. The same enthusiasm I have always had for teaching raced through me. Instead of thinking about how much of my salary I could bank, I thought about what it would take to help others create a pathway for success when struggling with debt.

I began thinking about the amount of money I had allocated for living expenses as I put every dollar I possibly could toward debt. If I had been living this way (carefully monitored budget) for several years, could I not continue to do so? Could I not "do without" the money I had been putting toward debt? My thoughts quickly returned to others experiencing life with debt. Stuck. Unaware, possibly, of behaviors or emotions holding them back. What was once my hope of becoming free of debt shifted to that of hope for helping others become free of debt. As a result, I created Puzzle Pieces to Pathway, LLC, with a mission to support others in the journey toward a debt-free life.

The *hope* of helping others.

Faith

****

Apparently, the quest for spiritual maturity is a lifelong endeavor.

-Andy Stanley
Deep and Wide (p146)
****

The beautiful, yet unexpected, "piece of the puzzle" for me was... and continues to be... my faith journey. Deep into the writing of this book, I became stuck. I froze. I questioned the need for integrating the story of my faith journey with that of my journey toward becoming free of debt. *Why? What was holding me back?* During my quiet time one morning in early May 2019, a realization hit me. I thought about recent conversations I had with family and friends. I thought about differences among churches, including those within my own community. I thought about the word, *community*, and the idea that the word holds different meanings for different people. (The root word, com, means together; in association with or completely.) *How could I possibly share my faith journey in a way that speaks to my readers- all readers? Would it be possible to share my thoughts and experiences about a shift in mindset from believing God's love is more about behaviors than that of a personal relationship with Him? Could I do this without causing others to feel offended or hurt?* The deeper I delve into my beliefs and understanding of faith, scripture, and love for others, the more I questioned my use of words in this section of the book.

Initially, the word, *hope*, was incorporated in my story to reflect my understanding of what it takes to begin managing finances responsibly (following decades of mismanagement) and the successes I encountered along the way. In the end, what I discovered was priceless. My faith journey paralleled my successful journey for getting out of debt. Along the way, my focus had been on paying off debt while becoming an active part of my community. My "dream" had been to owe money to no one- no person, no business- no one. I awakened to the fact that debt-free living held multiple meanings. Financial freedom. Freedom to live a life of helping others through struggles I had overcome. Freedom from burdens I carried because Christ died for my sins.

An Unexpected Faith Journey

I was thirty-one years old when I married. My husband, T, was thirty-three. I taught elementary school and he worked as an architect with a firm in Atlanta. We met in a Sunday School class at a church in Roswell, Georgia, the same church in which I was raised. A wonderful pastor. A church filled with friends and families we loved.

Our pastor married us in early December 1988. The church was decorated with fresh poinsettias in the windowsills and along the aisles, a beautiful Christmas tree covered in angel ornaments strategically placed next to the organ, and the familiarity of the sanctuary added a sensation of love and support. We thought our church, this special church, filled with family and friends, looked beautiful.

Soon after we were married, as many young couples do, we went in search of our "own" church where we could become involved as Mr. and Mrs. Our search did not take long. We found a church on the outskirts of Roswell where we were drawn to the pastor and ministers on staff. We quickly made friends with other couples and began serving in the youth department working with sixth, seventh, and eighth grade students. My middle sister and her husband were members of the same church. Our pastor, staff, and congregation were a close-knit group.

Months into our marriage, T came home from work one day and shared with me that he felt God's calling him into the ministry. I was surprised. Speechless. Shocked. Not because of the man he was, for he was a wonderful Christian man. Certainly, though, I was not a preacher's wife. I thought of such women as perfect or as close to perfect as a human can be. I was finishing my tenth year of teaching and was extremely happy with my work; loved my students and believed I was continually improving my role as classroom teacher each year. A teacher. Do you get what I'm saying?

Back to my initial reaction. *I didn't sign up to become a preacher's wife!*

To say the least, it was quiet in our home for the next several days. We were both trying to understand each other's thoughts and process the way in which our lives would change. I realize how selfish this sounds, as if all I cared about was my teaching job. It was more about the fact that I was afraid I wasn't worthy of assuming the role of preacher's wife.

The more I thought about it, the more open-minded I became. I wanted to support my husband. I could teach in any city. I had acquired experience teaching at the elementary and middle school levels. I truly loved my work and believed I could be happy teaching in any district in any state. I wanted my husband to be happy with his work. I embrace change. *How could I question what he believed to be God's calling?*

T began the application process and was accepted to study at Southern Theological Seminary in Louisville, Kentucky. I applied to school districts in that same city and surrounding areas. We put our house on the market, quickly had a sales contract, and were accepted into married housing at Southern. The move was happening! Giving notice, T resigned his position as architect, and I notified my principal and school district. We were preparing for a new adventure.

Within a few weeks, I was presented with an opportunity to interview with a school system in the Louisville area. When in Louisville for the interview, I would also be able to check out our married housing unit/apartment on campus to see where we would be living while my husband attended classes. T had not yet worked his final day as architect and had scheduled a follow-up doctor's appointment to discuss back pain he had been experiencing, but he wanted me to move forward with the interview even though he would not be joining me on this run to Louisville. Two of our friends offered to make the trip with me. We packed the car with luggage and a few things to begin making the apartment look homey. After we arrived and drove onto campus to check into the apartment, I called home to let T know we arrived safely and to find out what the doctor had to say. He said he would tell me about it when I returned home after my interview the next day.

Something didn't seem right. After pressing him for more information, I learned he had a tumor on his spine. My friends and I immediately jumped in the car and headed back to Roswell. They were so kind and comforting, offering to take turns driving through the night so I could get home more quickly.

When I returned home, T talked about further testing that needed to be done. As we scheduled doctor visits and made appointments for tests ordered by the doctors, we learned the tumor on his spine was only part of the health concerns expressed by doctors. The results of testing indicated cancer. Results indicated the cancer had already spread through his body, including his lymph nodes.

T was amazingly strong as we talked with the doctor about treatment he needed. We scheduled chemo and radiation treatments and overnight visits to Emory Hospital would soon begin. For those of you battling cancer or walking beside family or friends engaged in the fight, you know what is involved- both physically and emotionally- especially in the early days when you are still in shock.

We had sold our home. There were just the two of us, since we had no children. We rented an apartment in Roswell. Both of us had resigned our positions at work, so I quickly reapplied to Fulton County Schools. I scheduled an interview for a teaching position at Mountain Park Elementary School. Even though he had resigned his position at the firm, T's boss was empathetic and supportive. The official separation period had not lapsed, so his insurance coverage continued. This coverage was for T only. My previous teaching job had benefits. By this time, what we needed was to settle into our apartment and *hope* I would receive a job offer.

****

Special Memory

The evening following my interview at Mountain Park Elementary School, my mom visited T and me in our apartment. Mom and I were in the tiny kitchen washing dinner dishes as we talked with T seated across from us. As we were talking, the phone rang. It was the principal of Mountain Park offering me the teaching position! There we were, an apartment where T could rest to rebuild strength following treatments, and I was blessed with a job to support us, financially, during this time. My two sisters and their families, as well as my mom, lived in the area. Furthermore, Mountain Park, my new school, was not far from our apartment. I could be home quickly when needed.

****

T was strong in his faith, so he led our marriage with prayer and dedication. We attended our church and remained in the couples Sunday School class of which we had been a part. Most weeks, T could make it to church. He was becoming weaker, partly due to treatments and weight loss. After about a year of living in our apartment, we purchased a small cottage home in Alpharetta, a city bordering Roswell.

T's faith remained strong. He had, in my opinion, an extremely positive attitude as he continued battling cancer that spread from his colon to other parts of his body. Family and friends rallied around us. The faculty and parents of my students were overwhelmingly supportive. Not once do I remember T's complaining. Not once did he ask, *Why me?* He was a testimony for strong faith and belief in God's plan for each of us.

However, I did not know what to make of the situation. *Here is a man willing to respond to God's calling to become a minister yet unable to respond because he has cancer?*

****

Special Memory

It was mid-November 1991. We were a month away from our three-year anniversary. Hospice joined us in the fight and set up a hospital bed in our family room. T was weak. He was no longer eating. Instead, he was being fed intravenously. I was sitting in the chair next to his bed when I heard music... or singing. Christmas carols. I heard Christmas carols, yet it was early November. Nonetheless, it sounded like Christmas carols. I was confused because we did not have the tv or stereo playing. The sound was quiet except the faint sound of Christmas music. As the music sounded louder, I realized it was outside our family room window. I looked outside. There they were. Our Sunday School class gathered together singing Christmas carols. My heart melted. I walked outside and invited them in. Vividly, I remember everyone gathered around T, sitting or standing in the kitchen and family room. How special it was! What a beautiful memory!

****

On Thanksgiving eve, about a week after the Christmas caroling, my little sister and her husband offered to sit with T so I could get some sleep. Next to T's hospital bed situated in our family room, we had a large recliner. It held many a family member... many a friend... during that time. My brother-in-law came that night. It was comforting knowing someone who cared deeply for T was in the next room with him. The following morning, my brother-in-law greeted me with warmth and kindness and shared with me the news that T had slept throughout the night. My brother-in-law went home, and I sat in that same oversized chair. T looked peaceful as he lay asleep.

T passed away Thanksgiving Day 1991. Without a doubt, I know he is in heaven. Heaven. Free of pain. Free.

Returning to our house, after having left the house only hours earlier, my brother-in-law and sister came walking through the door. Family gathered later that day... sisters, mom, brothers-in-law, nephew... and I experienced added meaning to

Thanksgiving Day. This is one of the reasons I have enjoyed hosting Thanksgiving throughout subsequent years. This is a time when I think of family, friends, students, and parents who were there for us. In the hospital. In our church. In our home.

Pulling Away

Months after T passed away, I am not proud to say, I withdrew from the church we loved dearly and the life we had built together. After attending church together and serving together, walking into a church alone is difficult. It's as if I was part of a whole. At least, that's what it felt like. Church members were kind and inviting. My middle sister and her husband were members, so I was surrounded by loving faces. However, it was as if I was going to find a way to remove myself from the life of which I had been a part. I did not know in what direction to take my next step. I attended church sporadically. Different churches. Churches in the north Atlanta area.

I avoided managing my teaching salary responsibly. I was on my own to manage our home and the residual medical bills. I no longer wrote checks my husband and I placed in the offering plate at church. Life was different.

I had been blessed with a teaching career I loved since college graduation. Being in the classroom with my students seemed to be a source of great strength for me. With a strong desire to become more innovative and engaging as a teacher, I decided to attend graduate school. I could grow professionally, and it was a productive way to keep my mind occupied. I took out student loans for my master's degree and became excited about all I was learning, embracing the opportunities to apply what I learned to improve classroom instruction. After earning my master's degree, I moved into the curriculum specialist (CST) position, a position designated for each elementary school in the district. I thoroughly enjoyed this job, too. Working with amazing administrators, faculty, and staff serves as a strong foundation for a school-wide initiative. An added benefit is it came with a salary increase.

During the next couple of years, I continued to "church hop" and would go with family members to their churches on special occasions. It wasn't that my belief in God lessened. Instead, I invested my time and energy into my role as CST, supporting teachers, and working collaboratively with administrators, teachers, and parents to develop a school-wide initiative to provide enrichment for *all* students. My love of teaching continued to grow.

As stated earlier, my love of family runs deep. I loved my role as aunt. At the time, my middle sister and her husband had a son in elementary school and I thoroughly enjoyed spending time with him creating a nephew/aunt bond- a bond that exists today. Photos of such times together I genuinely treasure. The following November, my oldest niece was born. I could now look at the month of November as a birth and death month. A birth! The birth of my first niece! I had a nephew and a niece! I adored spending time with both. I was excited to become an aunt twice more as my little sister and her husband welcomed two other daughters into the world. What has always amazed me about my two sisters, among other things, is the way they "shared" their children with me. Being an aunt has brought a lifetime of joy! (Yes, parents, I know what you are thinking! You "get" to be an aunt- the fun job!) Believe me, "we aunts" recognize the hard work and investment you make as parents- the responsibility of caring for and guiding them throughout their teenage years! I promise! I get it! I understand. Not fully, certainly, but I do know how hard parents work! As a teacher, I have always tried to partner with parents and treat their children as "my kids." I admire and respect the role and responsibilities of parents.

Nephew and nieces, I had. Family, I had. Friends, I had. Teaching career, I had. However, I had no church home.

Five years later, after being introduced to a friend of one of the parents in my school, I married again. My husband was raised Catholic, and I had grown up in a Baptist church. Together, throughout the next few years, we occasionally visited different churches but did not become actively involved in any one of them. Because I had pulled away from church, I did not stress the importance of "church" when we met and dated. When we married, we never combined our paychecks. We kept our finances separate. The home where we lived was in my husband's name. He did a wonderful job making sure bills were paid and we shared some of the expenses, but we did not have a "joint" account, budget or financial plan. Thinking back, I may have been comfortable with separate accounts at the start of the marriage because I entered the marriage with student loan debt I accumulated while working on my master's degree.

The following year, I decided to return to college to earn a doctorate degree with the hope of one day teaching at the college level. Our finances remained separate, although we shared some expenses. Once again, I took out student loans for my doctorate and deferred the loans from my master's degree. Three years later, I completed the degree.

After five years of marriage, we divorced. It was hard. Really hard. Extremely hard. Knowing I have caused pain for others is the worst feeling- the absolute worst. For years, I could not say the word, *divorce*, as I was so ashamed. I know the ending was hard on our families, as well.

Finding My Way Back

Even though I believed in God and His love for me, I thought being a Christian was more about behaviors. If I "messed up," I wasn't worthy, especially if "The Bible says...." As a result, I thought about pulling away from the church completely. I was standing at a distance from God because I felt I had messed up so badly.

For a few months following the divorce, I lived in an apartment while the house I purchased was being built. In 2003, I moved into my home in Woodstock, a town not too far from my school in Roswell and began my 13th year teaching at Mountain Park ES.

The following year, I visited a large church in Alpharetta, one I had heard about from my neighbors. They were North Point Community Church Charter Members and had been a part of it (North Point) since its inception. What appealed to me at the time was the word, *large*. Perhaps the appeal was the *hope* of getting lost in the crowd. As emotional as I was about being divorced, I knew I would most likely become emotional during any church service.

Based on what I understood about the description of the church, there were two large auditoriums- the East and West. My neighbors commented the pastor usually spoke on stage in the East and the message was presented "live" on screen in the West. Knowing how difficult attending a service would be, I thought it best to go to the West. Greeters and ushers were friendly and helpful, but I decided to wait until the service began before walking into the auditorium. With the lights low, I could find a spot along the back wall and stand in the shadows.

During my first visit, I was surprised by the music. Growing up, I was accustomed to hymns, a piano, and an organ. Here, there was a band, concert-like lighting, and the words of songs presented on screens at the front of the auditorium. I listened. I read the words as they crossed the screen. I was too emotional, though, to sing. I remember listening to the message and thinking about how applicable it was to me. I don't remember the exact date of this first visit. I do, however, remember slipping out during the closing prayer, tears in my eyes, hoping to find my car in the large parking lot before anyone saw me.

I returned. I visited this same church again. I stood in the same spot along the back wall. I suppose I didn't feel I deserved a seat. Nonetheless, I was drawn to the church, the pastor's messages, and the large number of families in attendance. I told no one of my plans to visit. Instead, I slipped in after the service began and slipped out before it ended.

As I continued teaching during the next few years, I listened to teachers and parents talk about their churches. Even though I was drawn to the pastor's messages at North Point, something was holding me back. I began "church hopping" again visiting churches in the Atlanta area. I am not sure why. Perhaps, it was part of the healing process.

During my "church hopping" period, I returned to North Point Community Church between "hops." I was intrigued by the mission- *to lead people into a growing relationship with Jesus Christ*. In the field of education, school districts and universities have missions, local schools have missions, and many of us, as classroom teachers, have our own personal missions. But, a church with a mission. *Interesting*, I thought.

Enlightened

More frequently, I began attending North Point Community Church. One Sunday while singing with hundreds, thousands, of other attendees, a thought hit me! It was probably the teacher in me prompting my new perspective about the music portion of the worship service. Rather than thinking of the music/musicians as a band, I saw the musicians as Christians leading the congregation in song using their God-given talents and gifts. Until then, I "looked" at the music as a new style of church music, at least new to me, but that day I "saw" the musicians for the talented, enthusiastic, worship-leading persons they are! For those of you who may have experienced a change from traditional to contemporary church services, you may understand what I am saying.

I thought about the ways in which I tried to meet the needs of a wide range of learners in my classroom- some being musically gifted. It was no different with a group of adults. These musically talented Christians were expressing their love of God in song and engaging an auditorium of people in the process. Do you know what it's like to sing on Sunday mornings with such a large group of people? It's amazing! Talk about a sense of community!

From that day forward, I was in attendance. One Sunday, I *sat* in the West auditorium, as opposed to *standing* in the back against the wall as I had done in months past. I became interested in serving and knew there was an application process for the different areas of service, a step which certainly made sense to me. (In the back of my mind I had the looming question, *are divorced women allowed to serve? At church, would I be viewed as the same positive role model as in my role of classroom teacher?*)

Listening to Pastor Andy Stanley speak, I took notes each week and found his messages to be inspirational and challenging. In one of his series, "5 Things God Uses to Grow Your Faith," Pastor Andy challenged us to think about our confidence in God during pivotal circumstances. Of course, I thought about being divorced. Questions posed during the message included those associated with our confidence in God during these times. Did I pray? Did I pull away? I thought about the fact that I had moved from the back wall of the West auditorium to a seat in the West, embracing the music and thinking about the role God played in my life after my divorce. Along with the music, what I appreciated about this church was the way in which our pastor asked thought-provoking questions and made profound statements. The study of scripture, yes, but accompanied by the task of application. Growth. Spiritual growth. It was at this point I began to understand and personalize the church's mission- *to lead people into a growing relationship with Jesus Christ.*

What area of my life did I need to improve? *Finances.* I thought about debt. *My* debt. The pain debt caused. The pain from struggling with debt in silence. This pain was different from that of losing a loved one through death or divorce. People reach out to comfort those who have experienced loss. But, debt? *What do I do about debt?* This question surfaced among my many thoughts.

Not only did I take notes during the messages on Sundays, but also for the first time, I began to journal in the mornings before work and, often, again at night. My daily prayer became *Lord, help me to become an active part of my community.* In his series, "What Makes You Happy", I recall our pastor's words, "You were designed by the Giver of Live to give your life away." Was I giving of myself in *this* way? As a teacher, I lived this way. I continued to give of myself as a sister, daughter, aunt, and friend. I knew, though, there was more to becoming an active part of my community.

Stepping Out of My Comfort Zone

When I bought my home in Woodstock ten years prior, there was very little construction in the area. I purchased it due to its location, affordability, and size. My home was close to family and friends, yet situated between two colleges, hopefully one's being my future employer. One of the reasons I earned my doctorate in Curriculum and Teaching was that I hoped one day to teach at the college level. *If I loved teaching as much as I did, how wonderful would it be to work with future teachers?*

After more than 25 years with Fulton County Schools, it was time. It was time to move out of my comfort zone, to leave the school system to pursue a level of teaching unfamiliar to me- that of higher education. College. University. My only role at a university had been that of a student. If I wanted to teach at the college level and work with future teachers, the only way to move forward was to take the step- a step out of my comfort zone. I believed this to be true, but that action required a leap of faith.

My leap of faith was not only linked to my change to the university classroom, but also to my change in salary. My salary teaching at the university level, combined with my retirement benefits, was less than the salary I earned with Fulton County Schools. I had student loans, a mortgage, car loan, credit card debt, and credit union loan debt.

I made the decision. In the spring of 2010, I left my position with the school district, applied to teach at the university located slightly north of where I lived, and was hired to begin full-time teaching in August of that same year. The thought of working with college students- those with the dream of becoming teachers- thrilled me! I would be collaborating with professors in the field of education and preparing future teachers! Oh, yes!

Our church had been building satellite campuses, one

located in Woodstock a short distance from my house. Until construction began and was completed on the new building, the church held temporary services in the gymnasium of a nearby school. Plans for construction of the church had been developed, and the site was located even closer to me than the temporary site. As I thought about becoming involved in my community, I pondered whether I should I consider a move from the church in Alpharetta in which I had "taken a seat" and begun my personal spiritual journey?

I thought, *Do I visit the campus closer to my home or will that seem like "church hopping" again?* Knowing the pastor's messages were streamed inside and shared via the "big screen," it was comforting knowing the series/messages would be the same as those delivered in Alpharetta. Either way, I knew I had found a pastor, church home, and an opportunity to serve (when I "got the nerve").

As part of my quiet time, I continued with my daily prayer: *Lord, please help me and guide me to become an active part of my community.* In 2012, while attending Watermarke, the church campus in Woodstock, I began serving in the children's department working with the "crawlers"- the age between babies and toddlers. I loved it! Loved our room of crawlers. Loved the ladies with whom I served. Loved our captain and leaders in the children's department. Loved the fact that our group of volunteers in the crawlers' room chose to stay together over the next several years. Most of all, I loved the looks on parents' faces when they brought their children to our room and could see their children were happy to stay with us (volunteers) while they headed to the service. For those of you who are parents, you understand this. When you know your child is happy and cared for, it is much easier for you to leave them and enjoy the activity in which you are involved. For us (volunteers), we found great pleasure in knowing the parents could attend the church service as we cared for our sweet babies. I looked forward to this experience each Sunday. Family and close friends began asking, "How were your crawlers today?" I love it!

I continued serving in this capacity, taking notes during every Sunday service message. At home, I was engaged in quiet time in the morning and journaling daily. Often, my journaling centered around a thought-provoking statement or question posed during a message. I saw myself becoming an active part of my community... teaching at a local college, attending an incredible church, and serving in the children's department. My morning quiet time was comprised of reading, journaling, and prayer. Still, something was missing. What?

I was giving of *myself*- my heart. Was I giving of *all* my resources?

Think about it. Life. Work. Family. Faith. Friends. Housing. Food. Transportation. Entertainment. Not necessarily in this order, but each of us, I think, believes these to be important areas of life. So...*what* was missing? An area I should have seen years ago... no... decades ago. Finances. Money management.

Moving Forward

As a planner, one who appreciates working with a vision and paying attention to details along the way, I have thought financial management to be an area of strength for me. An area of interest. An area of success. Nonetheless, at this point in my life, I had only grappled with the concept of budgeting. I was proud of the fact that I had made monthly payments for ten years on a 30-year student loan. Ten years! Isn't that something? I had been in my house in Woodstock for those same ten years and only twice had I refinanced to take out the equity in my home to use for living expenses. Isn't that something? *No, not really,* I thought. As a result, there was little equity in my home after ten years of residence. And... the piles of debt existed.

This house served as my 13th residence since college graduation and I had lived here longer than any other home in my life.

For the past several years, I had been driving past a condo building on Main Street in Woodstock, the same town in which my house was located. When I first researched the prices of the condos at the time they were built, I found them to be too expensive to consider. Now, in 2012, following the downturn of the housing market, the prices had been reduced... significantly. There was a unit, a one-bedroom unit, that was affordable and comparable to the price I paid for the house where I was currently living.

Was it time? Time to make yet another move. Perhaps, as an investment this time? Speaking with a realtor, I put my house on the market and had an interested buyer within the week. The couple purchasing my home was moving from Florida to Georgia and planned to pay cash. My decision to move forward on the purchase of a one-bedroom condo was a quick one and within 45 days, I closed on the sale of my home and purchased the condo.

This condo is the same to which you were introduced in the first chapter, "The Dream." The condo on the top floor of a building overlooking Main Street, easy access to restaurants and shops, covered parking, and conveniently located near my church and the university campus on which I taught. This condo in which I lived for the next two years as I remained actively involved in my church, committed to teaching at the university, and growing in my faith. It was during this time I became serious about paying off my debt. (In the chapter, "Finances," I discuss the actions I took to become free of debt.)

I believed, however, "becoming an active part of my community" extended beyond living, working and serving in my community. I have been blessed my entire adult life with family, friends and a career in teaching students of all ages whom I adored and wanted to see flourish.

It was then I decided to alter my daily prayer to include, *Lord help me to live my life, so others see You through me.* My actions. My words. I knew what I was telling myself. Even though I believed I had always lived my life this way in the classroom and with family and when serving in the children's department at church, I knew I had not lived my life this way with respect to managing the money God had entrusted me. Had I been a giver to family? I believed so. Had I returned to the days when I tithed consistently. Not yet. I was giving, but not tithing. Had I accounted for every dollar every day? Hardly. Was it time to turn this area of life over to God and pray for his guidance moving forward? Absolutely.

Once again, a realization occurred to me. I wanted to live debt free. At this point, living a debt-free life meant something more than paying my debts. God sent His Son to pay my debts so I could begin a debt-free life. I made this connection and thought about what it means to give of my "whole self," including my resources- time, talent and money. This is the reason the title of my book was never a question in my mind. From the opening chapter, "The Dream", to current day living a debt-free life, my wish for others is to *Wake Up to the Dream of a Debt-Free Life.*

Hope, faith and love. The three are so tenderly connected. If my daily prayer is to live my life so others see Christ in me, then I wanted to reflect love for others in all I do. Thoughts. Words. Actions. I believe we are at our best when our thoughts, words, and actions are in harmony- each lifting others up- reflecting love and compassion. I created a phrase I think about as I prepare for the day. I begin the day by thinking **LOUD**ly. **L**ift **O**thers **U**p **D**aily.

I think about ways I can "lift up" those I will be meeting, as well as those I encounter throughout my day. (Often, this may be with a smile or laughter, as those who know me know I love to laugh.) I find it easiest to interact with others face-to-face because I can use inflection in my voice, facial expressions, and gestures to share my thoughts. Phone calls allow me to do the same. However, when communicating via email and text, I sometimes find it challenging to effectively communicate. You can only send so many smiley faces, hearts, thumbs up signs, etc. (Most likely, this is my "overly sensitive" side that leads me to wonder if the recipient understood my message as it was intended.)

Nevertheless, how can I move through my day of teaching, spending time with family and friends, and serving in my church and community with mismanagement of money/debt in the forefront of my find? How? With God's help.

As faith strengthens, we often see how God unravels problems, which in my case, was with the management of ... or lack of management of money.

Love

Love. Expressions of love and appreciation. Time spent with loved ones. Exploring ways to express love of family and friends- ways you can afford. Equating love and the amount of money we spend on someone seem disconnected; yet, so many of us desire to do all we can for those we love.

If you think about times when you were touched by love of family or love of friends, often the experience did not involve a great deal of money, if any at all.

I think about...

- The time our Sunday School class sang Christmas carols outside our home in November only weeks before T passed away. I felt loved and cared for by that special group of people.
- The joy I experienced through my sisters' and brothers'-in-law willingness to let me spend time with their children (my nieces and nephew) and be actively involved in their lives... from birth to current day.
- The incredible career in teaching and success with grad school fueled by my mom's neverending words of encouragement.
  (One of my favorite sayings as seen on my notepads and wall art reflects these sentiments. A mother bird and baby bird are looking at one another. The baby bird says, "What if I fall?" The mother bird responds, "Oh but my darling, what if you FLY?" -e.h.)
- The years my dear friend/colleague and I had had very little "extra" money when teaching together, so we surprised each other with a note and a box of Jr. Mints or Hot Tamales. Silly as this may sound, it was the simplicity of a token of thoughtfulness. She was a single mother of two young children; yet she made time to show her appreciation of our true friendship, one that has lasted more than 25 years. To this day, we reminisce about those days.
- The love, care, and support I have felt over the years when looking through boxes of letters/notes I have received from family and friends reflecting words of encouragement, expressions of love and appreciation.
- The deep friendship developed over decades with my dear friend of 50 years. As she lives in Florida and I in Georgia, to spend time face-to-face and catch up, we each drive to the "half-way" point and spend a day or two visiting and

sharing all that goes on in our lives (including that of our families). As a loving aunt, I could relate to her stories of motherhood. These special times are priceless as we continue our 50-year friendship.

- I experience the love and laughter when inviting friends to my home to share what goes on in our lives in the areas of faith, family, work, and play.
- The group of friends meeting to celebrate life events in each others' lives.

I could go on and on with list after list of what I love and appreciate about others. Most often, such experiences and memories are linked to time, designated time, spent face-to-face with others. Daily, I look at the photos displayed on a bulletin board I hanging in my home. You may have time during which you are present, time when your family and friends can "see" you want to be there. You, too, have probably shared such time.

When we are truly present in the moment, talking and laughing with loved ones, the experience can occur any place... at no cost, financially speaking. Being present. Listening. Caring. Loving.

Are there people in your life with whom you would like to spend more time?

Chapter 10

Purpose

****

You were designed by the Giver of Life to give your life away.

Andy Stanley
What Makes You Happy

****

God created the world on purpose. Each of us was created on purpose for a purpose. I believe each of us is uniquely designed to fulfill that purpose.

I thought, for me, purpose = teaching. As I have shared with you, I believed this was the area I "got right" and never questioned. However, purpose has become so much more to me now.

Our abilities and passion are from God. Finding and fulfilling our purpose, as I learned during my journey toward a debt-free life, involves more than "that one thing" in life.

For example, when I became serious about paying off debt, I was teaching in my "dream job" setting- that of a college classroom. Because I had always loved teaching, I thought about how wonderful it would be to work with future teachers. The college classroom environment allowed me to draw on years of teaching experienced I treasured. Working with these college students, combined with my belief in the conceptual framework on which the teacher education programs at the university were built, I could fulfill my purpose with enthusiasm and dedication.

Soon after beginning my work at the university level, I made the commitment to pay off debt. As outlined in the first few chapters of the book, I knew I wanted to no longer owe any company, agency or person so I began my journey toward paying off debt. No, it wasn't fun sticking to a budget month after month... after month after month. The chapters, "Facing the Truth" and "Taking That First Step," outline the steps I took to begin my journey toward paying off debt. Following a budget was challenging. However, as I accounted for each dollar I spent, my focus remained on teaching and serving. Instead of thinking about what I could not spend and how "deprived" I was because I changed my spending habits, I started each day by asking myself two questions.

1. *What can I do to improve myself to become the best I can be?*
2. *How can I utilize my talents and skills to make our world a better place?*

During 2014-15, I had reached the point of paying off debt with extreme vigor. As outlined in the chapter, "Facing the Truth," creating a "Facing the Truth Chart" is the first action I took to begin my journey. I listed each debt I owed, the agency or company owed, the total amount owed to each, and the minimum payment due each month. I extended my chart to include a record-keeping sheet to record the amount I paid to each agency monthly, including any extra I paid, and recorded the "new balance" of each debt. I kept my "Facing the Truth Chart" in front of me. I reviewed it every day. I kept it in my "I Can Do This" space (discussed in the chapter, "Organization").

At the same time, I was deeply involved in my work at the university creating my promotion and tenure binders with the goal of going up for tenure in 2017-18. One of the areas of tenure was service to school and community. Being an active part of our campus, at-large, was important to me. Challenging? Yes.

Meaningful? Absolutely. Service to community, in my mind, incorporated service within my church community. I had been serving in the children's department, specifically in the "crawlers" room, and had also become interested in women's ministry- perhaps in the role of a small group leader.

I began to "see" my purpose through different eyes- the way God sees me- the way He sees each of us. I began to think about the skills, talents, and gifts of those around me- individually and collectively. When fully utilized, our talents and skills allow us to serve a greater purpose than I ever could have imagined. I never questioned whether I was designed for the field of education but moving to the college classroom setting I believed had been a gift from God. His doing. His guidance. Even though I was committed to my work on campus and thoroughly enjoyed working with colleagues and students, I not only thanked God every day for my position on campus and the opportunity to work with future teachers, but also for family, friends, home (apartment), health, and involvement in my community. Practicing gratitude was a daily practice.

In 2016, as the thought of leaving my position as dean and creating Puzzle Pieces to Pathway surfaced, I realized, without having planned for it, areas of my life had merged.

- Passion for teaching merged into my role as dean
- Responsible budgeting and accounting for the money I earned merged into responsibility for oversight of school budget
- Focused work on promotion and tenure merged into service in my community, including my church community in various capacities

In his book, *How to Manage Your Money*, Larry Burkett wrote, "If as Christians we can accept our role as stewards and manage God's resources according to His direction, He will entrust us with even more. But why would He entrust more of His property to us if we hoard and act like owners? When we acknowledge God's total ownership, we can experience God's miraculous and wise direction in all areas of responsibility, including financial management" (p19).

Throughout my journey toward a debt-free life, my most profound realization of all is the fact that **the more I gave of myself and my money, the greater success I had paying off debt!** Yes, you read this statement correctly. It's true! The more I gave of myself and my money, the greater success I had paying off debt.

To this day, I can hear the voice of my pastor, Andy Stanley, say, "You were designed by the Giver of Life to give your life away." These words are powerful. From the moment I heard them, these words resonated with me.

****

We make a living by what we get.
We make a life by what we give.

Winston S Churchill

****

Each of us has a purpose. With purpose often comes growth.

At the beginning of the chapter, I wrote the phrase, purpose = teaching (in my life). As I grew and evolved, I found the "puzzle piece," purpose, developed greater significance. Yes, teaching, in my mind, *is* service. But there are countless capacities in which we serve. Teachers. Parents. Wives. Daughters. Sisters. Aunts. Friends. Ministers. Mentors. Leaders. Business owners. Small group leaders. Authors. Artists. You name it. We all have a purpose.

I am touched by the words of Paul, "And since we have gifts that differ according to the grace given to us, let each exercise them accordingly" (Romans 12:6).

As we work together to make our world a better place, we can be extraordinary.

For me, the decision to pay off debt led me through an unexpected faith journey. My pathway toward a debt-free life was a path that led me closer to God. Last year, I remember seeing a magnet in a gift shop last year displaying a picture of a red heart broken into several pieces and the phrase, "When Your Heart Is Broken, Give All the Pieces to God, "written below the broken heart. *My sentiments, exactly.*

It's interesting. When I became free of debt in November 2016, I thought I would have reached my "final destination" so-to-speak. Love of family and friends. Career. Health. Involved in church and community. Zero debt. At that point, I would be able to continue in my role as dean, save money (lots of money), volunteer, and live the "dream life." Instead, my spirituality was awakened.   I believed there was more. More to serving my purpose.

****

What material success does is provide you with the ability to concentrate on other things that really matter. And that is being able to make a difference, not only in your own life, but in other people's lives.

-Oprah Winfrey

****

Chapter 11

Purpose Beyond Comparison

What can be wonderful about fulfilling our purpose in life is the connectivity such an aim produces. You may be living a life of purpose in the role of parent, spouse, leader, sister, daughter, aunt, friend, grandmother, minister, caregiver, entrepreneur, mentor, accountant, teacher, nurse, restaurant server, sales associate, student, job search or perhaps, you are currently engaged in change within your neighborhood, church, or school community. You have been thinking about becoming more actively engaged in service. If so, then this chapter may speak to you.

Regarding area(s) of service, you are perhaps filled with enthusiasm about your passion- be it working with children, volunteering with community charities, tutoring, mentoring. Or, you may be seeking to develop your personal passion.

See the beauty of life! It's not too late. As our seasons of life change, though circumstances differ among us, most of us want to experience security and significance. Security, for most of us, includes financial security- being free of debt. Significance, for many of us, is linked to purpose.

My experience interviewing people of different ages, from a variety of walks of life, strengthened my belief that we need to be careful not to judge others. Appreciating others contribute to our world can lead to connectivity. Connectivity, not comparison. Comparing your life, your purpose, your circumstance to that of others may generate negative feelings. These feelings may hold you back from accomplishing what you hope to do. For example, if you are interested in becoming free of debt, but, like me, you struggle in silence and can't seem to take that first step, you may be thinking, "Sure, she was able to get started. She had a job she liked and probably earns a decent salary." What you don't know about the person you reference is the amount of debt for which she is responsible, the number of people for whom she is responsible, the amount of help she may or may not receive, financially speaking, and the support she may or may not have in her circle of family and friends.

Furthermore, when we compare our lives to those of others, we do not have the full picture. Many of you who are busy parents with hectic, demanding lives think life would be perfect or easier if you were single, had no children, or had children grown and completely on their own. You, who are single, without children or family, may long for family meals, lots of noise in your home, trips to the ballpark, game night at home or a family outing. In her book, *Comparison Trap*, Sandra Stanley writes, "There is no win in comparison. And there's no love in comparison either." How can we love, support and encourage one another when we are busy filling our minds with what love is not, such as jealousy and envy? Does it really matter that our friend's chip-n-dip bowl used during a football game gathering is cuter than the bowl we use with our friends and family? Will anyone remember the outfit "we just had to have" for an event two years from now? What others will remember is the way we treated them. Did we love and encourage? Did we use our strengths to support those around us?

Just as we learn to manage our money, so it is with our lives- our resources, abilities, and natural God-given talents- to pursue our purpose and support one another. I have heard the expression, people come into our lives for a reason, a season or a lifetime. We may enter another person's life for a specific reason, an encounter that lasts for a short period of time. In other cases, we may cross paths with others to support them (or have them support us) throughout a difficult transition in life. This connection may look different when we see one person's life as opposed to another. We can remind ourselves the way one of us supports another may help differently. We want to be careful to extend a hand but not set expectations for others' actions regarding their support. We don't always know what is in the pipeline for their lives. No two people are exactly alike. Only you can do what you were designed to do. Let's all put our best foot forward along the pathway created for us. If each of us strives to make the world a better place, think of our collective, positive impact. These beliefs- this mindset- served as the springboard for my creation of Puzzle Pieces to Pathway.

As I shared with you earlier, a habit I have found meaningful is the habit of thinking **LOUD** (ly): **L**ift **O**thers **U**p **D**aily. I think about how I can lift others up through a letter of appreciation, phone call, note, message, or face-to-face conversation. There are so many around us contributing to make our world a better place in ways we appreciate, recognize or hear about through others. Think about how good it feels to you when someone lifts you up, then pass that feeling along- or pay it forward.

I think about the 85-year-old woman who, after retiring from the Atlanta Center for Disease Control, serves on the board of directors for her condo building and organizes activities in which residents can be involved.

I think about the pastor who, through meaningful messages and sharing of God's word, encourages his congregation and inspires them to engage in service within the church community.

I think about husbands, heads of household, leading their families with love and faithfulness.

I think about the young parent providing a loving

environment for her young child as she finishes school and begins a career.

I think about the special education teacher partnering with a gravely ill parent to provide the best education possible for the child.

I think about the warm, kind-hearted young lady serving as a receptionist at a conference center as she welcomes guests and works to organize their lodging and meeting spaces.

I think of the intelligent young man working to support his father's business in the area of technology.

I think of today's youth managing time spent connecting electronically, and handling emotions associated with their observations.

I think of special friends who have been beside me through happy times and sad.

For each of these, among many others, I strive to "lift up" daily... in some way. Letters of appreciation, phone calls, notes, messages and face-to-face conversations are affordable! Thinking **LOUD**ly is priceless!

****

Special Memory

When I first struggled with finding ways to show others I care, ways I could afford, I began writing personal notes and letters to them. These were not simply thank-you notes. These notes were written with the intent of highlighting what I appreciated most about them and sharing with them the positive impact they have had on my life.

The powerful impact of note writing occurred to me in 2002 when I was working as CST at Mountain Park Elementary School. One of the teachers and her husband wrote a note to me and enclosed a gift card to a restaurant I enjoy. As much as I appreciated the gift card, it was the note they had written that touched my life.

Oct. 31, 2002

Dear Cindy,

A few weeks ago I told Jim about how supportive you have been to me and to everyone, really, at mta. Park. Realizing that you are the one always giving to others, we decided to do something for you outside of school. We wanted to encourage you and treat you to something special, so we thought of a gift certificate to Macaroni Grill.

Thank you for modeling professionalism and commitment and leadership with such a servant heart. You are highly respected and should be shown appreciation more often. You

look out for us teachers, stand-
up for us and what is practical
in the classroom, and are
always willing to do anything
to ease our load.
　　Thank you so very much,
　　　　　Sincerely,
　　　　　Louise

Cindy,
　　Here's my 2¢ worth: You'll never
know how much all your efforts
mean to Louise. She is constantly
coming home to say what you have
done to help her, and how you
have lightened her load. So by
your kindness to her, you help our
whole family! What a blessing you are.
We are both grateful to you.
　　　　　Your friend,
　　　　　Jimmy R (the great)

P.S. Listen to the CD
on getting some margin in your life.
(But you can have butter at the macaroni
　　　　　　　　　　grill)

This note, this powerful heartfelt note, meant the world to me at a time when I was going through a divorce, without a church home, and inexplicably unaware of the full extent of my struggles managing finances. Even though these areas of life presented challenges, I never stopped pouring myself into family, teaching, and the two questions I ask myself daily: 1) What can I do to improve myself to become the best I can be? 2) How can I unitlize my talents and skills to make our world a better place?

More than fifteen years following the receipt of this note and placement of it in my Bible, I attended THEOPRAXIS at North Point Community Church. By this time, I was involved in a small group, free of debt, and actively working to launch Puzzle Pieces to Pathway, LLC, as a way to help others begin the journey toward a debt-free life. As I walked into the room, there they were. Louise and Jim were seated at a table near the door! I sat with them to catch up. As the session began and our group started talking, it seemed appropriate to mention the note Louise and Jim had written so many years ago. After all, I had my Bible in hand with the note tucked inside. I didn't read the note to our group, but I talked about the profound impact the words had on my life and emphasized the power of words.

****

To this day, I carry special notes, letters, and cards from my sisters, mom, nieces, nephew, friends, colleagues, and students not only in my Bible, but also my daytimer and computer bag. Furthermore, I post notes received on my refrigerator and bulletin boards hanging in my home and store them in easily accessible photo boxes in my home. What a joy it is reading through these cards! Don't we all enjoy reading such notes? Like the people who gave them to us, they are *priceless*.

Is there someone in your life to whom you would like to express love or appreciation with a few written words? Perhaps a family member, child's teacher, community volunteer, doctor, dentist, close friend, new friend, pastor, neighbor?   Let me tell you, without a doubt, it feels as good writing a note as it does receiving one. I carry blank note cards with me wherever I go. If I am waiting for an oil change, dental appointment or the start to a meeting, for example, I spend a few minutes writing a card to someone I know. Always, such a gesture gives *me* a lift! Who doesn't enjoy receiving a note through U.S. mail. Real mail. Ah! Are you with me? Again, the powerful impact of words! *Priceless.*

Chapter 12

Relationship

At the onset of the creation of Puzzle Pieces to Pathway, LLC (PP2P), I named this "puzzle piece," *Fashion*. A deeper dive into thoughts and conversations about fashion, shopping, and the wide range of reasons *for* shopping led to the name, *Relationship,* instead.

****

Who looks outside, dreams; who looks inside, awakes.

-Carl Gustav Jung

****

Spending Habits

Do you have a favorite movie? For most of my life, *The Sound of Music* has come to mind when I identified my all-time favorite movie. I am certain some of you are thinking, "Wasn't that a move from the 1800's?" My nieces, "bless their hearts," watched it every year when they stayed with me during the Christmas season. As young girls, they enjoyed it, provided I "fast-forwarded" through a song or two. Now, as they have finished college and started their careers, we can laugh and reminisce about the special times by looking at photos, instead of watching the movie.

However, I think it was some time in the period, 2011-2012, my favorite movie changed to one quite different. *Confessions of a Shopaholic* became my "go to" movie. Google offers the following summary:

Like many New York City gals, Rebecca Bloomwood (Isla Fisher) loves to shop. The trouble is, she shops so much that she is drowning in debt. Rebecca would love to work at the city's top fashion magazine but, so far, has not been able to get her foot in the door.

I didn't necessarily connect with Rebecca's need to shop, but I certainly related to her situation... "drowning in debt." I remember watching the movie and laughing at the way she managed her credit cards, charging to the limit on each. At one point, as a strategy for curtailing her use of a credit card she promised herself she would no longer use, she placed it in container of water and froze it. When she took the block of ice out of the freezer for an "emergency" shopping trip, she frantically chipped away at it with the heel of an expensive shoe.

At one point, a friend of Rebecca's asks, "Why do you shop?" She responds by saying, "When I shop, the world gets better. And then it's not." She continues by explaining her need to shop again. It's a cycle. The world gets better (while shopping), and then it's not (when facing debt).

Can you relate? Retail therapy? Perhaps not to such a dramatic scenario, but have you tried to stop using a credit card? Have you put it away or "hidden" it from yourself as an attempt *not* to use it?

In the end, Rebecca decides to sell everything she owns- clothes, shoes, handbags, scarves, gloves, accessories- and use the money to pay her debts, an act she does in full. It was her journey, however, that intrigued me. I could relate to so many of the emotions she was experiencing. I could relate to feeling so overwhelmed in the beginning, a feeling leading to a sense of hopelessness. Seeing her tenacity inspired me. Silly as this may sound, the character in this movie inspired me. I was inspired to rethink spending and think about tackling debt.

Clothes are "fun" for my two sisters and me. As I made the decision to tackle debt, I made a personal decision look at *my* wardrobe differently. I no longer thought, *I don't have anything to wear.* Instead of thinking how nice it would be to have something new to wear, I decided to repurpose the items in my closet.

Let me share with you how this came about. I was flipping through a magazine when I saw an outfit that I liked... a lot. (To this day, I think about a point made by my pastor during a Sunday message. Awareness fuels discontentment. Certainly, looking through apparel magazines can fuel an unnecessary "need" for clothes!) As I looked more closely at the photo, however, I realized I had the very same items hanging in my closet- a denim shirt, sweater, pin, jeans, and boots. However, it had not occurred to me to put the items together in such a way. I tore out the page of the magazine and posted it on a bulletin board in my office. That was it. That was the moment I decided to stop buying clothes. Instead, when I came across a photo of clothes I liked, like those in my closet, I would pair my already purchased items in a way I had not previously considered. Does this make sense? Soon after I tore that photo from the magazine, I came across others. To this day, I have the bulletin board of photos hanging in my closet as a reminder of this mindset and a reminder of this part of my journey toward debt-free living. (Please, remember your taste in clothes may differ from mine based on your age, personal style and/or taste.)

By the way, the picture of the three little girls is a photo of a piece of art hanging over the piano in our home when I was a child. I always thought of the picture as representing my two sisters and me. (It's *not* their clothes! Simply their closeness.)

"Fashion Board"

(A change in mindset... instead of flipping through magazines to look for items I wanted to purchase, I began looking at photos for ideas… ideas for repurposing what I owned. It worked!)

One woman I consulted during a Puzzle Pieces to Pathway session asked me to help her with the "puzzle piece," Relationship. She was not struggling with debt but was interested in working on her closet. It was filled with clothes… and I do mean *filled*. She said she often shops and, without realizing it, purchases an item like what she already has in her closet. Furthermore, she shared it was difficult to let go of some of her favorites even though she has not worn them in years. In her closet, she housed a range of sizes and held onto them just in case she needed them.

We worked together for five hours, non-stop. She was so excited to take a deep dive into her closet and assemble outfits. This experience for her is like my experience cutting out photos from magazines or sale flyers. Look and appreciate what you have and "repurpose" the items hanging in your closet.

During my interviews with people of different ages, backgrounds and marital status, a theme emerged when talking about spending money unnecessarily. Often, a shopping trip, be it on foot or online, took place when the person was lonely due to need for relationship, sad because there were too few friends in their lives, or anxious about current circumstances or an upcoming event stemming from lack of self-esteem or poor relationship with self. The shopping and purchasing stemmed from an emotion. Each time, the emotion was linked to relationship, or lack of.

Questions and declarations I heard included, but are not limited to, the following:

- "I'll feel better if I have a new outfit for the occasion."

- "The school year is starting soon. I want my children to feel good as the year begins. Their friends will have new clothes. I am just going to buy a few things."
- "My wife shops. I golf. Both are expensive, but it makes us *feel* better."
- "This is an incredible sale. I can't afford *not* to buy it!"
- "Lottery tickets aren't *that* expensive. All it will take is the "winning ticket."
- "Life is challenging right now. I'll feel better if I plan a girls' get-away. I just need to get away from my problems for a few days."
- "In my line of work, I need the latest tech gadgets. It's important in my circle of colleagues."

When listening to these comments and engaging in conversations, I did not hear them say they *needed* new clothes (or other items); instead, they needed to "feel good" about themselves, their lives, or the way they cared for loved ones.

Pursuit of Contentment, Not Pursuit of Things

This is particularly difficult in our world of social media. One scroll through profiles and photos displays beautiful homes, clothes, cars, offices and people. Trying to "keep up" can be costly. Considering today's "virtual mall" and easy access to "stuff," it has become habit for many to get caught up in the cycle of assessing what others have, reacting by spending to "keep up," then becoming frustrated with mounting bills from unnecessary spending.

Have you purchased something and immediately felt buyer's remorse? Have you taken time to examine the feelings around *why* you bought the item? Was the *buying* more important than the *having*?

In the chapter, "Purpose," the concept of connectivity is discussed. In most of us, there exists a strong need to connect with others. During a NPCC Women's Night Out event in March 2018, I heard Shasta Nelson speak to a large audience of women. As I usually do when I am inspired by a speaker, I took notes and, later, referenced my notes when talking with friends or small groups of women.

Shasta Nelson spoke about the continuum of relationship (friendship). She coined the term, *frientimacy*, as the experience of a meaningful friendship; a heartfelt, supportive closeness among friends. The use of this term supports the belief that we are wired to connect with one another. She expanded on the use of this term during her presentation by talking about three areas she believes need to be incorporated into a relationship- positivity (balance of giving and taking in the relationship), consistency (time together), and vulnerability (sharing/letting more of us be seen). Shasta Nelson spoke about these three terms in the context of a triangle with positivity serving as the base.

I share this with you because I believe we are all different in what we need most. Some of us need laughter. Others need affirmation or a listening ear. If we are void of such positive experiences or without friendship/relationship, many of us seek other ways to be "filled." Shopping. Shopping online. Spending. Spending money on things we do not need. Many of us shop or spend money to fill a void in our lives. The void may exist as a result of a separation from family due to a career move, a divorce, a move to another city after finishing college, or a void resulting from long hours of work connected only to your computer or mobile device. For whatever reason, at any age, many of us shop and spend in place of connecting with people.

How does this relate to finances or living with debt? Those

struggling with debt understand the emotions and stigmas often associated with debt- emotions that generate a sense of embarrassment, shame, frustration, or hopelessness. We all experience negative emotions but the reasons for them may vary from person to person. In her book, *Frientimacy*, Nelson states, "Our goal isn't to avoid all negative feelings in our lives; that's impossible. Pain, disappointment, sorrow, and frustration are all part of what it means to be human, so they'll be a part of our relationship experience, too" (p 34).

Throughout my journey to a debt-free life, I began replacing spending *money* with spending *time* with family and friends, as well as serving and volunteering in my community. In the chapter, "Facing the Truth," how many of you identified "eating out" as a category of unnecessary spending? Replacing eating out with a different activity that costs little or nothing, not only saves money, but also provides an opportunity to connect with others. For example, I began meeting friends at a nearby walking trail and walking four miles while talking and "catching up." This activity led to money saved and life-enriching outcomes- a healthier me and a deeper level of friendship. One-on-one "facetime," real facetime, is a gift. Priceless. For you, this may involve strolling a grandchild as you take a walk, meeting a friend after work to walk and talk, picking up your child after school and going for a walk together to hear more about the school day, or taking a walk with your spouse or significant other after dinner. If you live alone or have moved to a new city, finding a nearby park where you can spend time outdoors and be around people may enhance your life in a way scouring the internet for things to buy never will. Wherever you are and whatever you are doing, spending time outside and spending time with others is much more enriching than spending money.

As you are reading, some of you may be thinking, "I am too embarrassed to be around people. What if they find out I am struggling with debt? What if they think less of me because I do not have more than I do?" This is the beautiful part about connecting. As we spend time with others, sharing and letting more of ourselves be seen, we learn that everyone has an area of life he or she would like to improve.

I listened to the video, "The Greatest Speech Ever," by Oprah Winfrey. She spoke about the beauty in the fact that each day is a new day we have been given. How we start the day and carry ourselves through the day is a choice. Choices we have made led us where we are. Are changes needed? Today, we have another chance to do better and to become more of who we were created to be. As I listened to Oprah speak, I thought about the two questions I ask myself each morning.

1. *What can I do to improve myself to become the best I can be?*
2. *How can I utilize my talents and skills to make our world a better place?*

For so many years, I knew one of the answers to the first question. Take action and tackle debt! For so many years, nevertheless, I avoided this call to action. Is this an area you need to improve? If you are reading this book and made it this far, you are serious about living a debt-free life or helping someone you know live a debt-free life. You may be reading to find out what this "wake up to a debt-free life" is all about before you make the decision to act. You may have scanned the titles of the chapters and wondered, "How can there possibly anything wonderful about the journey to be debt free?" By this point in your reading, I have introduced you to several life-enriching outcomes, including the action to make connections, be it reconnecting with friends or developing new relationships.

Most of us are searching for happiness and contentment. I found the steps I took in the pursuit of faith, love, perseverance, godliness and kindness to be life changing. I want the same for you. For this reason, my mission with Puzzle Pieces to Pathway is to reach out and invite you to join the journey to a debt-free life.

Chapter 13

Finances
&
Giving

In 2011-12, if you had asked me my plan for paying off the massive amount of debt I had accumulated, I would not have been able to give you a clear answer. I could pay my bills. My income was at its highest. I contributed to a 403b systematically. It seemed as if all was well and, for the most part, all *was* well. Or, so I thought.

Why did I wait decades to manage my money responsibly? I truly believe it stems from the fact that I had not embraced the concept of people as managers of money. We did not enter the world with money. We can't take it with *us*. While we are here on earth, we are managers of what has been entrusted to us.

"The earth is the Lord's, and all it contains, the world, and those who dwell in it" (Psalm 24:1).

As a Christian, I accept my role as manager of resources from God. I now see this to be the case, not only with my money, but also my time, talents, and gifts.

I have never been afraid of hard work or long hours, to say the least. I have worked at least two jobs most of my life. Why? I did not manage the money I earned- the money entrusted to me to handle wisely. Instead, I spent what I earned… and then some. If I didn't have it to spend, I took out a loan. Did I spend only on myself? *Absolutely not*. Did I spend only on "stuff?" *Certainly not*.

Did I spend to earn advanced degrees? *Yes.* Do I regret it? *No.* Could I have handled grad school without student loans if I had learned earlier in life how to better manage money? *Oh, yes!*

There are countless resources on the topic of finances available to us. There are experts in every field from debt to building wealth, insurance, stock market, and becoming a millionaire. Why, then, according to Forbes, as of August 2019, Americans' outstanding student loan debt stands at $1.6 trillion and credit card debt stands at $870 billion? I believe this is largely due to the lack of education in the area of financial literacy. As adults, we moved through our youth and into adulthood developing poor spending habits and mismanaging finances. Along the way, we developed negative emotions about our financial status. Many of us reached a point when we felt *hopeless* when considering a "way out."

We become frozen. Stuck. Circling in a pattern of inaction. We believe we are alone, so we struggle in silence... month after month, year after year. This is the good news! You are **not** alone. You can do this! You, too, can set a goal to become free of debt. Instead of "seeing" this goal as a process, consider it a journey- a journey filled with life-enriching outcomes along the way. This is the reason I chose to create Puzzle Pieces to Pathway, LLC and write *Wake Up to the Dream of a Debt-Free Life*. I gained far more than I sacrificed during the journey. The joy of unexpected life-enriching outcomes led to a sense of freedom and contentment I never knew possible. I want the same for you.

****

Since you get more joy out of giving joy to others, you should put a good deal of thought into the happiness that you are able to give.

—Eleanor Roosevelt

****

Coaching and mentoring people in their 20s, as well as those in their 50s and 60s, I found actions that led to success include:

- Creation of a "Facing the Truth Chart"
- Development of a budget
- Designation of each dollar earned to a specific category
- Prioritization of giving/tithing "off the top"
- Procurement of a second job (or side hustle), if additional money is needed
- Record-keeping of every dollar spent
- Communication with those impacted by your budget
- Focus on your giving of time, talent, and money as a part of life
- Engagement in the community through volunteer work
- Application of every dollar possible to debt outlined in their "Facing the Truth Chart "
- Investing in personal and/or professional growth

You *can* do this. As you continue reading, do so with the attitude, *I can do this!*

In his book, *How to Manage Your Money: An In-Depth Bible Study on Personal Finances,* Larry Burkett discusses how God uses finances. He states, "Often God uses money in our lives as a means of direction, because it is an area in which most of us are sensitive and vulnerable. If we are open to it, He promises to supply His wisdom and direction. But His plans for us are not always the same as our desires. So, we must be willing to accept His plan." (p21)

Just as each of us is unique, our pathways for success are unique. Your pathway may look different from that of mine, a neighbor, friend, or family member committed to becoming free of debt. But to become successful, we must respond to the call to action. Creating a plan, developing daily habits in support of that plan, and focusing on life-changing habits every day allows us to move in a positive direction.

As I write this final chapter of *Wake Up to the Dream of a Debt-Free Life*, I have numerous documents and books in front of me. Each one holds significance in my journey to be debt-free. Countless times throughout my journey to be debt-free, as well as during the writing of *Wake Up to the Dream of a Debt-Filled Life*, I picked up each of these books and files. The list of books is alphabetical. For me, the impact of the combined list is profound. I am grateful to the authors of each.

Awaken by Priscilla Shirer

Are You Fully Charged? by Tom Rath

Believe to Achieve by Brian Tracy

Better than Good by Zig Ziglar

Comparison Trap – by Sandra Stanley

Daily Reflections for Highly Effective People
        by Stephen R Covey

Deep and Wide by Andy Stanley

The Essential Wisdom of the World's Greatest Leaders

Edited by Carol Kelly-Gangi

Frientimacy by Shasta Nelson

How to Manage Your Money by Larry Burkett

Irresistible by Andy Stanley

Jesus Lives by Sarah Young

Leadership Fitness by Homer Rice

Louder than Words by Andy Stanley

The Magnolia Story by Chip and Joanna Gaines

Make Your Mark by Coyte G Cooper

The Millionaire Next Door by Thomas J. Stanley and William D. Danko

Mindset by Carol S. Dweck

New American Standard Bible (Reference Edition)

The Seat of the Soul by Gary Zukav

The 7 Habits of Highly Effective People
    by Stephen R Covey

The Total Money Makeover by Dave Ramsey

Your Best Year Ever by Michael Hyatt

Women and Money by Suze Orman

People of all ages, races, religions, and backgrounds are struggling with debt. The journey to be debt-free involves learning and growing in many areas of life. A calculator can handle the mathematics of the "process," but our hearts hold the emotions associated with the journey.

Moving from the mindset of "controlling spending" to "managing money entrusted to you by God" is quite a feeling! It's freeing. Remember "the dream" in Chapter 1? Waking up to the "dream coming true" is an expression I used to describe my journey.

For me, reading books and listening to speakers who, in my opinion, are "game-changers" in our world- those striving to lead others to live their best lives possible- challenge me to learn, grow, and improve every day.

Remember the two questions I ask myself each morning?

1. *What can I do to improve myself to become the best I can be?*

2. *How can I utilize my talents and skills to make our world a better place?*

I understand some of you believe you do not have enough time to read. I get it. Work, family, and life consume the hours of our days. Sometimes, however, waking up 3o minutes to one hour earlier to set aside quiet time to read, meditate, and reflect before your day begins is well worth the sacrifice of those minutes of sleep. In today's world of technology, some of our most influential speakers and leaders record presentations or post podcasts for our listening pleasure as we drive, walk or ride to work.

I thought it may be interesting to you, the reader, to gain insight into the role print played in my journey to a debt-free life. By now, based on your reading of this book, you understand my use of the term, debt-free, holds multiple meanings.

Earlier in this chapter, along with books I read throughout my journey, I also mentioned documents I referenced during this time. For the past decade, I took notes during services at North Point, Watermarke, and Woodstock City churches and reviewed these notes often. I journaled daily so I have journals filled with thoughts and experiences during my journey to a debt-free life. Together, with my tattered red folder (referenced in several chapters), bank statements, and my Federal and State Individual Income Tax Returns for the years, 2002-2018, I was able to assemble detailed facts and figures to chronicle my story for this book.

You now have a sense of what I found to be instrumental in my quest to help others. As you can see, not only do we need a calculator, pen and pencil, or a laptop, but also resources to support and encourage us throughout the journey to be debt free. Resources include, but are not limited to, sermons, books, articles, videos, live speakers, documents, family members, and friends.

I have learned from the best of the best through reading, reflecting, relationships, and prayer. Listening to messages delivered by Andy Stanly and reading books he has written played a significant role in my faith journey. Reading books written by experts in the field of money and finance, such as Zig Ziglar, Dave Ramsey, Suze Orman, Thomas Stanley and William Danko assisted me in my journey to become financially free. Studying the work of Drs. Carol Dweck and Coyte Cooper led me through a period of personal growth as I transitioned from teaching at the university level to creating and developing Puzzle Pieces to Pathway with the *purpose* of helping others.

Sure, there are books containing proven steps taken for becoming debt free. There are books recommending insurance policies you should hold during each season of life. There are books written to serve as guides to lead you through the process of investing in the stock market, purchasing real estate, or building wealth. How wonderful it is we live in a country with resources at our fingertips- resources to help us learn and grow!

What you may need, as was the case for me, is support and encouragement to take the first step. Taking the first step is personal. Taking the first step is emotional. I get "it" (living with debt). I do. I lived *it*. I survived *it*. The beauty of it all is I experienced life-enriching outcomes along the way.

My purpose for writing the book is to reach out to you, and others, and let you know you are not alone. You are not alone in your journey. *Wake Up to the Dream of a Debt-Free Life* was written to help you create a pathway for success toward becoming free of debt. For this reason, you may find it helpful to revisit or reread several chapters of *Wake Up to the Dream of a Debt-Free Life,* including "You Know You Want To," "The Fearless Step," "Facing the Truth," "Purpose," and "Purpose Beyond Comparison." You may also find the questions and resources included in *Wake Up to the Dream of a Debt-Free Life: A Personal Guide* may serve you well.

At this point, you have been reading, reflecting, and thinking about what your journey toward a debt-free life could look like. When I started my journey, I tried to do the same but had no idea there would be such wonderful experiences and outcomes as a result of what I thought would be a difficult, demanding, lonely journey. Challenging? Yes. Habit changing? Certainly. New approach to managing money? Absolutely. Clearer understanding of the phrase, debt-free life? Without a doubt. A more peaceful, joyful life? An unexpected outcome of the journey!

Let me "paint a picture" of what the start to my journey looked like. I...

- Began each day with a morning quiet time filled with devotions, reflection, and gratitude.
- Established a place in my home, referred to as my "I Can Do This" space as described in the chapter, "Organization."
- Charted the total amount of money I owed (debt) on my "Facing the Truth Chart," as outlined in the chapter, "Facing the Truth."

- Created a budget and designated each dollar I earned to a category listed on my budget sheet, including the category of debt, as discussed in the chapter, "The Fearless Leap."
- Included giving as part of my budget and moved toward automated online giving.
  (As part of my "Facing the Truth," I pulled my Income Tax Returns for the years, 2003-2018. I charted the amount of money I earned, my charitable contributions and my "tithe." Growing up, I was taught from an early age to tithe- give 10% of my earnings to support the church. In the chapter, "Hope, Faith, and Love," you read about what happened to my giving as I was "church hopping." What I found most interesting when assembling these documents and charting the contents was the more I gave, the more money I had to pay off debt. During the years I tackled debt with vigor, 2012-2016, I was consistently tithing. Moving from the mindset of "controlling spending" to "managing money entrusted to me by God" is quite a feeling! It's freeing. Remember "the dream" in Chapter 1? Waking up to the "dream coming true" is an expression I use in this book to illustrate years of navigating aimlessly before the start of my journey to a debt-free life.)
- Determined the total amount of money needed to pay the minimum amount due to each agency/company listed on my "Facing the Truth Chart."
- Revisited my budget sheet (often) to look for ways to cut the amount of money designated for each category, including the possibilities for cutting categories.
- Contacted several insurance agencies to identify the most cost-effective agency and policy for auto and home.

- Lived on a tight budget (income from pension for years of service with school district) and applied all income earned from my work at the university to the debt I owed.
- Took on additional courses to teach, providing additional income.
- Made the decision to increase the amount of money I applied toward debt, so I took on a Saturday job… a "side hustle" as many refer to it… and applied earned income to debt.
- Sat down in my "I Can Do This Space" daily and made notes about day-to-day spending, current balances in each category listed on my budget sheet and possibilities for continually adding to the amount of money I applied toward debt. Key word… *daily*. I reviewed my budget sheet, "Facing the Truth Chart," and notes… *daily*. (Once I started paying off debt and experienced the feeling of a $0 credit card balance, it felt better than any new dress, handbag, or latest tech gadget. I kept at it! Every day. Consistently. With dedication. One credit card at a time!)
- Sold my condo in 2015 and applied equity to my student loan debt.
  (I do not recommend this for every person. However, when owning a home and paying a mortgage, I developed a bad habit of taking out home equity loans or second mortgages to pay debts and I would redecorate, spending money unnecessarily. However, I had *not* changed my spending habits, so I ran up credit card balances again and still had a second mortgage payment. I purchased my condo at the downturn of the market so when prices began to rise, I sold it and moved into an apartment. I knew I would be spending long hours working on campus in the dean's role, so I made this decision. Besides, the *size*

of a house doesn't make it a *home*. I moved into an apartment with rent falling into my budgeted 20% of income. *Note: Saving is a part of my budget and the decision to purchase a home may be in my future. If so, I will not purchase a home and be "house poor.")*

- Cancelled cable and gave away my tv, one of the best decisions I made.
- Continued to put forth my best effort at work. At the time I was offered the dean's position, I knew I had developed responsible decision-making habits and strategies for managing money with which I was entrusted. I had "mastered" budgeting and developed skills to prioritize needs and document spending.
- Made time for friends and family, be it a phone call, face-to-face conversation over a cup of coffee or meeting to walk the trails while catching up.
- Continued to engage wholeheartedly in my role at the university, making myself available to faculty and students.
- Attended church services regularly at Woodstock City Church. After my move, and as of today, I attend North Point Community Church.
- Volunteered weekly in Waumba Land (children's department for infants through Pre-K) serving in the "crawlers" room for approximately five years.
- Joined a NPCC women's small group and began to learn more about Women's Community Groups and leadership.
- Participated in events and sessions at North Point Community Church designed for volunteers, leaders, and future leaders of small groups.
- Wrote letters of appreciation to those who have impacted my life and did my best to outline the reasons for the special roles they played in my journey.

For some, it was through personal relationships. Others, as authors, speakers. or as meaningful role models.

- Prayed daily for focus, strength, and wisdom to become who God designed me to be... in *all* areas of life.

Today, as this book goes to print, I am experiencing what it means to live a debt-free life, both spiritually and financially. As a result, I am happy to have the freedom to develop Puzzle Pieces to Pathway, LLC with the mission to support others in the journey to debt-free living.

****
"If therefore the Son makes you free, you shall be free indeed."

John 8:36
(New American Standard)
****

To this day, I think about my fears at the start of my journey. My thoughts of others experiencing these same or similar fears serve as the springboard for my work with Puzzle Pieces to Pathway, LLC (PP2P). It is the life-enriching outcomes of the journey I wish for you. From the bottom of my heart, I wish for you the freedom I now experience.

You *can* do this. Join me... join others... in the journey to a debt-free life.

* *

We don't just find our brave and survive the storms for ourselves, God designed us to live in community so that our experiences can help others. People all around us are looking for help as they navigate the challenges, and we can demonstrate a victorious way of living, even in challenging times.

-Holly Wagner
Find Your Brave: Courage to Stand Strong When the Waves Crash In

* *